YOUR
INTRODUCTION
TO REAL ESTATE

YOUR
INTRODUCTION
TO REAL ESTATE

DAVID M. LIEBERMAN, B.A., M.B.A., J.D.
Chairman, Department of Business
Western Piedmont Community College
Member of the Bar, State of New York
Licensed Real Estate Broker, State of North Carolina

VNR VAN NOSTRAND REINHOLD COMPANY
NEW YORK   CINCINNATI   ATLANTA   DALLAS   SAN FRANCISCO
LONDON   TORONTO   MELBORNE

Van Nostrand Reinhold Company Regional Offices:
New York   Cincinnati   Atlanta   Dallas   San Francisco

Van Nostrand Reinhold Company International Offices:
London   Toronto   Melbourne

Copyright © 1979 by Litton Educational Publishing, Inc.

Library of Congress Catalog Card Number: 78-26148
ISBN : 0-442-24790-7

Manufactured in the United States of America

Published by Van Nostrand Reinhold Company
135 West 50th Street, New York, N. Y. 10020

Published simultaneously in Canada by Van Nostrand Reinhold Ltd.

15   14   13   12   11   10   9   8   7   6   5   4   3   2   1

Library of Congress Cataloging in Publication Data

Lieberman, David M.
    Your introduction to real estate.

    Includes index.
    1. Real estate business. I. Title.
HD1375.L5   333.'3   78-26148
ISBN 0-442-24790-7

TO MARION

who made it all possible

About the Author . . .

David M. Lieberman holds a B.A. degree from the University of North Carolina at Chapel Hill, an M.B.A. degree from Adelphi University, and a J.D. degree from St. John's University Law School, and is chairman of the Department of Business at Western Piedmont Community College in North Carolina. He teaches business law, real estate, and insurance. He is a member of the Bar of the State of New York, and a licensed real estate broker in the State of North Carolina. His previous work experience includes a private law practice. He is a member of the American Business Law Association, the Southern Risk and Insurance Association, and the Rotary Club.

TO THE READER

You are about to embark on a journey of learning—one that I believe will be interesting as well as informative.

This book is *not* intended to be a totally comprehensive text; it *is* intended to be a concise, readable survey of the important aspects of Real Estate for those who wish to learn about this fascinating subject, whether to help prepare for a licensing examination, as part of formal course study, or simply for their own satisfaction. From this starting point, you will perhaps be encouraged to broaden the scope of your study.

The problem in a book of this type becomes one of "selective cutting"—where to trim material, so that readers may be spared the task of wading though details they neither wish nor need, yet avoiding the mistake of omitting valuable information.

Much time has been spent in attempting to tread this fine line between excessive wordage and incompleteness. I hope that this objective has been achieved, and I would welcome comments from those who have suggestions as to how the presentation of the subject matter might be improved.

David M. Lieberman

ACKNOWLEDGMENTS

A substantial portion of this book was completed during a period of leave from Western Piedmont Community College, Morganton, North Carolina, during which time I was associated with a local real estate and insurance organization.

To that "local organization"—The Norvell Company of Morganton, North Carolina, Real Estate and Insurance Brokers, goes my deep appreciation for their cooperation during my stay.

David M. Lieberman

CONTENTS

YOUR
INTRODUCTION
TO REAL ESTATE

1.

FUNDAMENTALS OF REAL PROPERTY

THE NATURE OF PROPERTY

What is "real estate"?

Basically, it is land, something we all are familiar with and readily visualize. Fine, you say, but what about things *on* the land—a house, for example? The answer is that real estate includes not only the land but anything permanently affixed to it, either a man-made improvement (the house) or something that is growing naturally on it (a tree).

Real estate (or "real property") may therefore be defined as land and its appurtenances (the things that are part of, and go along with it).

We distinguish real property from personal property. The simplest way to understand the difference is to think of personal property as anything that is not real property.

Interestingly enough, it is possible for something that is personal property (a section of pipe, for example, lying in the plumbing contractor's warehouse) to become real property by being installed in a house. Anything so "affixed" loses its character as personal property and becomes part of the realty. We call such items *fixtures*.

Is it possible for the reverse to take place, so that something that is part of the realty can lose its character as real property, and become personal property? Certainly; think of a tree that is cut down and removed. By severing it from the realty we have changed its character from real property to personal property.

It is not always easy, however, to decide whether certain personal property has become part of realty, and would therefore be automatically included in a sale of that realty. In doubtful cases, where no agreement

1

between the parties has been expressly stated, various tests are sometimes used as a guide. For example, what was the *intention* when the object was installed; was it intended to become part of the realty?

Another test might be whether the object could be removed without substantially damaging the realty, or even the object itself.

Generally, personal property that is reasonably needed in the use of the real property would be considered real property, even though not permanently attached physically; an example might be window screens in a dwelling.

You have heard this phrase jokingly applied to land: "They're not making any more." This statement is, of course, true. Land is a relatively scarce commodity, which explains why, particularly in densely populated areas, growth must be primarily upward rather than outward.

Another characteristic of land is its uniqueness. Regardless of similarity, no two parcels of real property are "substitutable" for each other. This uniqueness has important implications in matters involving contractual obligations affecting land. As you may know, in the typical lawsuit the complaining party asks for money damages to compensate for another's failure to fulfill some obligation. In matters of real estate, however, the subject of the agreement is "unique" and therefore money damages might not constitute adequate compensation for the aggrieved party, since he cannot "substitute" some other parcel of real estate for the one wrongfully not transferred as promised.

To illustrate, suppose a valid contract exists between Mr. B the buyer and Mr. S the seller of a house and lot. Mr. S breaks his agreement. Mr. B, because real estate is unique, can sue Mr. S, not for money damages, but for what the law calls "specific performance"—a remedy calling for the court to compel the defendant (Mr. S) to fulfill his contractual obligation. (Awarding Mr. B money damages would probably not be adequate compensation since no other house and lot is "substitutable" for the one in his contract with Mr. S.)

INTERESTS IN LAND

Now that we have an idea of what real estate is, we should examine the concept of *rights* in real estate. Let us start with *ownership*.

All of us own some things—a car, wrist watch, refrigerator. To own something is to have rights in that object which the law will protect against interference with our possession and/or use of that object. In real estate we refer to that ownership as *title,* and we refer to a property owner as one who "holds title" to the property.

While it is true that the law will protect these rights against others, this "ownership" is not without limitations. You cannot use your property in such a way as to cause harm to another; government may impose regulations covering the use of the property, and may tax your ownership. Further, under what is called the right of *eminent domain,* government has the right to acquire your property for some public purpose, so long as you are paid adequate compensation for it. The process by which government acquires your land is called a *condemnation proceeding*.

Bearing these limitations in mind, let us consider the scope of ownership in real property. Traditionally, ownership not only includes the surface of the property, but extends upward to the heavens and downward to the depths of the earth. Of course the owner cannot prevent airplane travel, since the law permits this, but he does own the "air space" above his land, subject to that right of air travel. Similarly, minerals lying beneath the surface are part of the real property, and the right to them would go with the land in a transfer of ownership, or the mineral rights could be sold separately, or retained by the seller of the property.

If property borders a stream or lake and the owner has the right to use the water, we say that he has *riparian rights*.

All of this seems simple enough, but not all ownership is the same. There can be different degrees or "quantity" of ownership, and these are referred to as *estates in land*.

The extent to which you have rights in land determines the particular estate you have. There are two broad categories of estates. One is called *freehold estates,* and refers to ownership. The other, *non-freehold* (or *leasehold*) estates refers to something less than ownership. The latter concept will be examined in the discussion of Landlord and Tenant.

Let us consider only the following two freehold estates:

FREEHOLD ESTATES:
   FEE SIMPLE ABSOLUTE
   LIFE ESTATE

The fee simple absolute (sometimes referred to merely as the "fee") is the highest quantity of ownership one can have. Subject only to the limitations we mentioned earlier (the rights of others and governmental power) the owner of the fee enjoys unrestricted possession and use of the land forever; this means that (1) the property may be transferred by him; (2) it may be inherited from him by others; (3) there is no time limit to his ownership.

The *life estate,* although it is ownership, is limited in time. The ownership exists only for the period of someone's lifetime. For example, A might give ownership to B for the period of B's life; or he might give ownership to B for the period of C's life.

The life estate, therefore, may be measured either by the life of the grantee (the one to whom ownership is being given) or by the life of some other person.

The obvious question now arises—what happens to the land when the life estate terminates because of the death of the one whose life measures the time of ownership? The answer to this question points out the chief difference between a life estate and the fee—the fact that a life estate generally cannot be inherited. Upon its termination, ownership reverts back to the original owner (or his heirs, if he has already died).

It is possible for a grantor (one who transfers ownership) to give a life estate and provide that upon termination, ownership is to go to a third party rather than revert to the grantor. To illustrate, A grants a life estate to B for B's life, and provides that upon B's death, ownership is to go to C.

Assuming that B later dies and C is now the owner, what estate does C have? Interestingly, it is not a life estate; no such language was used. C has a fee simple estate.

The holder of a life estate (or *life tenant,* as he is called) may transfer the property, but remember—the duration of the estate will be governed by the length of life of the person originally designated. As a general rule of law, one cannot convey to another any greater interest than he himself has. As an example, if A grants B a life estate, and B transfers the property to C, C holds only a life estate measured by the life of B.

The life tenant is entitled not only to possession of the land, but also to any income from it. But he is under an obligation not to commit what is called *waste,* which would consist of any conduct on his part that would damage the interest of the one who will be the subsequent owner (for example, failing to pay real property taxes, changing the character of the land from one type of use to another, etc.).

There is a situation in which a life estate may be created by "operation of law," which is a phrase used to describe a condition under which, because of some statute, something is brought about automatically without any particular action by any individuals. Most states, for example, have statutes providing that upon the death of a married person, his or her spouse has certain rights in the real property of the deceased.

In many states the surviving spouse has the right to elect to take a life estate in one third the value of all real property owned by the deceased at death. Obviously, if the surviving spouse stands to inherit a greater proportion than this, either by will or otherwise, this statutory right is of no significance. But in a situation where the deceased's will left little or nothing to the surviving spouse, that spouse could take a life estate in one third of the deceased's real property, regardless of what the will provided.

With this in mind, you will now understand one good reason for having the wife of a grantor join in the deed of a transfer. Without her signature, there would exist the possibility that at some later time she, or someone claiming through her, might assert a statutory right to a portion of the property transferred.

CO-OWNERSHIP

It is possible for two or more persons to have a simultaneous interest in the same property. Any estate in land may be held this way, and it is referred to as "concurrent ownership." The persons who are co-owners are called co-tenants.

We will consider the three most common forms of concurrent ownership: joint tenancy, tenancy in common, and tenancy by the entirety.

Joint Tenancy

In joint tenancy, each of the co-tenants is considered as owner of the entire estate in the land; there is no dividing of portions. There exists the "right of survivorship," which means that upon the death of one co-tenant, his interest passes to the surviving co-tenant or co-tenants, and *not* to his heirs.

Some states, including North Carolina, have statutes stating that joint tenancies in real property do not carry the right of survivorship unless as expressly contracted. In other words, in such state, if A and B own land as joint tenants, and there is no provision for the right of survivorship in the contract or deed, upon the death of A, his heirs (*not* the surviving co-tenant B) will receive his interest.

For a true joint tenancy, there must exist what is known as the "four unities" of time, title, interest, and possession. This means that the interest of the joint tenants must be one and the same interest, it must have been acquired at the same time and by the same deed, and the possession must be undivided.

This raises an interesting question. Suppose property owner Jones marries and wishes his wife and himself to own the property as joint tenants. He thereupon executes a deed to himself and his wife as joint tenants. However, since Jones had already owned the land, the unities of "time" and "title" did not exist—the ownership of Jones and his wife did not arise at the same time and under the same instrument. A technicality such as this could mean that Mr. and Mrs. Jones would have a co-ownership other than as joint tenants (such as tenancy in common, which we shall examine next). However, in an attempt to eliminate this undesired result, many states now have statutes which enable a present property owner to create a valid joint tenancy by deeding to himself and another "as joint tenants."

A joint tenancy is not indestructible. If, for example, Brown and Green are joint tenants, and Brown conveys his interest to Smith, thereafter Green and Smith own as tenants in common; the joint tenancy has been destroyed.

If husband and wife own property as joint tenants, and are subsequently divorced, does this destroy the joint tenancy? Since state laws vary on this question, the result would be determined by the law in the particular state.

Tenancy in Common

Here the co-tenants own fractional interests in the property. These interests are undivided, but they need not be equal, and need not have been acquired at the same time. Each co-tenant may freely sell his interest, and the buyer would then become a tenant in common with the other co-tenants.

Should there be disagreement among the co-tenants as to whether to sell the property, any co-tenant may bring a court action for *partition,* following which there will be a court-ordered sale, and the proceeds will be distributed among the co-tenants.

There is no right of survivorship; upon the death of a co-tenant, his interest passes to his heirs.

In many states, where land is transferred to two or more persons, and there is no specific language indicating the type of co-ownership, a tenancy in common will be presumed.

Tenancy by the Entirety

This is a special type of co-ownership, applicable only to husband and wife. It carries the right of survivorship, so that upon the death of either spouse, the survivor becomes the sole owner of the property. Since neither spouse can defeat the other's rights by selling or mortgaging the property, it is necessary that both husband and wife sign any documents relating to such transactions.

What if a husband and wife, who own property as tenants by the entirety, become divorced? Since tenancy by the entirety is limited to the husband-wife relationship, divorce converts this type of co-ownership into a tenancy in common.

A transfer of property to a husband and wife will create a tenancy by the entirety unless the document clearly indicates that some other form of co-ownership is intended.

Community Property

Some states (mostly those with a Spanish, rather than an Anglo-Saxon heritage) recognize the concept of *community property*. In these states, any property acquired by either husband or wife while they are married belongs to them both, as co-owners. This is so, even if the property is in the name of only one. Under this concept, each spouse is considered to own an undivided 50% interest in the property, and there is no right of survivorship; that is, if one spouse dies, the survivor receives only his or her 50% interest. Any heirs of the deceased spouse would receive the other 50%.

Property acquired before marriage does not become community property; nor does property acquired by a spouse as a gift or inheritance, even during the period of marriage.

States recognizing community property include Arizona, New Mexico, Nevada, California, Washington, Louisiana, Idaho and Texas.

Condominiums and Cooperatives

Much has been written and discussed in recent years concerning condominiums and cooperatives, probably reflecting the desire of many Americans to have some benefits of home ownership with few, if any, of the burdens of property maintenance.

The basic difference between condominiums and cooperatives lies in the type of ownership. In a condominium, the occupant of the dwelling unit actually is the owner in fee simple of that unit. For such ownership to be valid, it has been necessary for states to enact statutes legalizing it, since you will recall that in our previous discussion of title to real property we emphasized "land" and the vertical ownership of it (from the depths of the earth to the heavens). In the case of condominiums, we are thinking in terms of horizontal, rather than vertical ownership.

The condominium owner makes his mortgage payments and pays his real property taxes like any homeowner. These taxes, together with his mortgage interest, are deductible on his income tax return. As to the land and the other portions of the building he shares with the other owners in the multi-unit development, all of the condominium owners are tenants in common.

In a cooperative, it is not the individual occupants of the dwelling units who own those units. All the land and improvements are owned by a corporation which has probably financed the ownership largely by mortgaging the property. It then sells stock in the corporation to prospective residents who, by their stock purchase, become entitled to occupy their respective units on a long-term basis.

The occupant's monthly payment is determined by the amount the corporation needs to cover its total operating costs, including taxes and mortgage payments. Each occupant is therefore responsible for his proportionate share of the corporation's obligations.

While the cooperative also offers the benefit of income tax deductions for mortgage interest and real property taxes, the basic difference between the cooperative and the condominium should be obvious: a condominium owner is relatively "insulated" against the fates and fortunes of his neighboring condominium owners. In the cooperative, on the other hand, the ability of his neighbors to meet their obligations to the corporation might well affect his future monthly assessments, since it is ultimately the occupant-shareholders who are responsible for meeting the corporation's obligations.

A government publication draws the following comparison between condominiums and cooperatives:

COMPARISON OF SIMILAR TERMS

	Cooperatives	Condominium
Mortgagor	The cooperative corporation.	Each individual owner that borrowed money to purchase the unit.
Mortgagee	The lending institution.	Same.
Monthly Charge	Proportionate share of all costs including mortgage.	Percentage of common estate costs. Any mortgage payments on the individually owned unit are paid separately as are those assessed on the individual unit.

	Cooperatives	Condominium
Real Estate Taxes	Assessed on the property of the cooperative corporation.	Assessed on the individual unit.
Voting	Each member has one vote.	Each owner has the number of votes representing the percentage of value of his unit to the total of all units.
Mortgage Term	Cooperative corporation usually has 40 years—member is not a mortgagor.	Owner usually has 30 years—condominium is not a mortgagor.
Closing or Settlement costs	Costs in addition to the price of the corporate property including mortgage service charge, title search, insurance and transfer of ownership charges paid when the cooperative first purchases the property. Only a small transfer fee is charged to transfer future membership in the cooperative.	Costs in addition to the price of a unit and its undivided interest in the common estate including mortgage service charge, title search, insurance and transfer of ownership charges paid each time the unit is resold or refinanced.
Equity	Increase in the value of a membership certificate over and above the initial or "downpayment" resulting from members' monthly contribution toward payment of the corporate mortgage.	Increase in value of ownership interest in the unit as the owner pays off his mortgage and from market value appreciation.
Escrow Funds	Subscription or downpayments required to be held unused until the viable cooperative is assured. Transfer of membership funds are sometimes escrowed until the transfer is complete.	Subscription or downpayments required to be held unused until the condominium regime is recorded on the property and titles are conveyed to each buyer. Escrows are usually used in each resale situation. The deed is held in escrow until all conditions of the sale (including any prepayments) have been met.

At this point we should mention another type of land interest called an *easement*, although it is not ownership. An easement is not one of the "estates in land" to which we have referred; it is simply a right to use another's property for some particular purpose. A common example would be a right of way across your neighbor's land.

If A and B are adjoining property owners, A might grant to B the right to cross A's land at a particular point, in order that B may have access to a certain road. Note that A is not granting ownership to B; he is merely giving him an easement, the right to use.

We call this type of easement an "appurtenant easement," because the right to use becomes appurtenant to the land; it is said to "run with the land," so that if B should sell his property, the new owner would have the right to cross A's land, just as B did.

An interesting illustration of easements is present in a *party wall* situation. A party wall is an outside wall that straddles the line dividing two properties, and is used in common by both property owners. Since the center line of the wall is on the property line, each owner has an easement in that half of the wall lying on his neighbor's property.

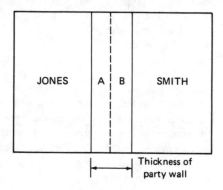

In the above illustration Smith has an easement in "A" and Jones has an easement in "B."

It is possible for a property owner, without granting an easement, merely to give someone the right to come onto the property for some temporary purpose. This is called a "license." The issuance of a ticket to a sports stadium or theater is an example of such a license. A license may be granted verbally, but in any event is personal (it does not run with the land), cannot be transferred, and is revocable.

Another interesting question arises in cases involving *lateral support* with regard to adjoining property owners. The phrase "lateral support" refers to the support which the soil of a landowner gives to the land of an adjoining property owner. If A, by some activity such as excavating on his property, causes adjoining owner B's land to collapse because of the withdrawal of this lateral support, A is liable to B for damages. But this is true only if the damage was caused to B's property in its natural state; if the collapse took place only because of the weight of the structure, A would not be liable to B unless he was negligent in the excavation, and B can prove that, with proper care, the damage would not have resulted.

Some state and local laws provide that, where an owner contemplates excavation, he must notify adjoining property owners, and must take specific steps to protect the land and structures of those adjoining owners.

TRANSFER OF TITLE

As we saw earlier, the word "title" is used to denote ownership. The owner, or holder of title, derived his ownership from a previous owner, or title holder. If we were to trace back the ownership of a particular parcel of real estate by searching the records, we could determine the ownership at any prior time, so long as the written records go back that far.

The concept of private ownership of land developed from grants made by a sovereign government to individuals. As these individuals made subsequent transfers of their property, a "chain of title" was created, and it is this chain that is reflected in what is called a title search. Someone making such a title search will thereby develop an *abstract of title,* which is an outline of the history of ownership of a particular property, referring not only to the deeds of ownership, but also to any other recorded instruments (documents) which have affected that property—mortgages, for example.

The chief purpose of a title search is to make sure that the present owner holds a title that is free of "clouds." A cloud on title might exist where there is something in the record indicating the likelihood of someone other than the record owner having some claim to, or interest in, the property. You can therefore understand why, when a transfer of ownership of property is contemplated, a title search is done in order to assure that the owner is able to transfer what is called *clear* or *marketable* title.

It may come as a surprise to you to learn that title to real property may be transferred *involuntarily*—in other words, against the wishes of the owner. But before we proceed to that unusual phenomenon, let us consider some of the usual ways by which title is transferred voluntarily.

FORM 17-A. ATTORNEY'S CERTIFICATE OF TITLE   Printed and For Sale by James Williams & Co., Inc., Yadkinville, N. C.

To:

Attorney's Certificate of Title

I hereby certify that I have examined the public records of the office of the Register of Deeds and the Clerk of the Superior Court of _____ County, North Carolina, with reference to and investigating the title to the property of _____

and, in my opinion, they are seized of a good and sufficient title in fee simple, so far as is disclosed by the records, to the following tract of land:

except the following incumbrances and irregularities; and subject further to any variation in description which an accurate survey might disclose:

This the _____ day of _____ , 19____ .

_____ , Attorney__ .

By _____

Final Certificate of Attorney

I hereby certify that all exceptions listed in preliminary certificate shown above have been properly cancelled of record, or removed, and that conveyance recorded in Book _____ , Page _____ , Filed _____

_____ , to _____

_____ for $ _____ constitutes a first and prior lien on the property described, so far as is disclosed by the records, subject to any irregularities in description that an accurate survey might disclose.

_____ , Attorney__ .

Date _____   By _____

Deeds

Conveying ownership by executing a deed is the most common method of transferring title. By statute, certain transactions must be in writing to be legally enforceable. One such statute is the transfer of an interest in real property, which invalidates the oral deed. The old phrase "Signed, sealed and delivered" is particularly appropriate to deeds. In fact, a deed that is not delivered does not operate to transfer title, even though it is complete in every way.

The deed must name the parties (the grantor and grantee), it must recite consideration (although the exact selling price need not be given), and it must contain a description of the property.

Deeds traditionally contain an acknowledgment somewhere at the end of the document. This section is a declaration before a notary public (or similar officer) acknowledging that the execution of the deed is the free and voluntary act of the person signing (the grantor).

The acknowledgment is not required by law. However, to record the deed it is necessary that it be acknowledged, and since it is most important that it be recorded, having the acknowledgment is a virtual necessity.

Why is the recording of the deed so important? Simply because an unrecorded deed would probably be void if some innocent party acquired an interest in the property, unaware of the existence of that deed.

To illustrate, suppose Adams deeds property to Baker, who does not record the deed. Adams later deeds the same property to Cummings who knows nothing of that prior sale. Cummings promptly records his deed.

Even if Baker thereafter records his deed, as between Baker and Cummings, the innocent purchaser (Cummings) has good title. Baker may have legal recourse against Adams (if he can find him) but as to the property in question, Cummings has good title, even though his deed bears a later date than Baker's. What is important is not the priority of time in the execution of the deed, but the priority of time in the recording of it.

The time of recording takes precedence because the purpose of recording any instrument is to give notice to the world of the rights conveyed by that instrument. If the holder of such rights fails to protect his interest by giving notice of them, he is making it possible for some innocent party to be misled.

There are several different types of deeds, but only those most commonly encountered will be considered.

We all are familiar with warranties in various types of transactions. The warranty guarantees or promises something, and warranty deeds do the same—they guarantee that the grantee will not have his possession and use of the property disturbed by someone claiming an interest in the property. The *general warranty deed* makes this guarantee, and the grantor giving this type of deed is thereby promising to protect the grantee from any such claims, regardless of how or when such claims arose. A typical general warranty deed is shown on the following two pages.

A somewhat narrower protection is contained in the *special warranty deed*. Here the promise is to protect the grantee against any claims originating during the grantor's ownership, that is—against claims arising out of some act of the grantor.

Excise Tax	Recording Time, Book and Page

Tax Lot No. .... Parcel Identifier No. ....

Verified by .... County on the .... day of ...., 19...........

by ....

Mail after recording to ....

....

This instrument was prepared by ....

NORTH CAROLINA GENERAL WARRANTY DEED

THIS DEED made this .... day of ...., 19........., by and between

GRANTOR	GRANTEE

Enter in appropriate block for each party: name, address, and, if appropriate, character of entity, e.q. corporation or partnership.

The designation Grantor and Grantee as used herein shall include said parties, their heirs, successors, and assigns, and shall include singular, plural, masculine, feminine or neuter as required by context.

WITNESSETH, that the Grantor, for a valuable consideration paid by the Grantee, the receipt of which is hereby acknowledged, has and by these presents does grant, bargain, sell and convey unto the Grantee in fee simple, all that

certain lot or parcel of land situated in .... Township, ... County, North Carolina and more particularly described as follows:

N.C. Bar Assoc. Form No. 3 © 1976

The property hereinabove described was acquired by Grantor by instrument recorded in ....

....

A map showing the above described property is recorded in Plat Book .... page..........................

TO HAVE AND TO HOLD the aforesaid lot or parcel of land and all privileges and appurtenances thereto belonging to the Grantee in fee simple.

And the Grantor covenants with the Grantee, that Grantor is seized of the premises in fee simple, has the right to convey the same in fee simple, that title is marketable and free and clear of all encumbrances, and that Grantor will warrant and defend the title against the lawful claims of all persons whomsoever except for the exceptions hereinafter stated. Title to the property hereinabove described is subject to the following exceptions:

IN WITNESS WHEREOF, the Grantor has hereunto set his hand and seal, or if corporate, has caused this instrument to be signed in its corporate name by its duly authorized officers and its seal to be hereunto affixed by authority of its Board of Directors, the day and year first above written.

-- ....(SEAL)
                    (Corporate Name)

By: ....(SEAL)

....President

ATTEST: ....(SEAL)

....Secretary (Corporate Seal) ....(SEAL)

USE BLACK INK ONLY

SEAL-STAMP   NORTH CAROLINA, COUNTY OF ....

Use Black Ink

I, ... a notary public of said county do

hereby certify that ....

.... Grantor,

personally appeared before me this day and acknowledged the execution of the foregoing instrument. Witness my

hand and official stamp or seal, this............... day of................................., 19.........

My commission expires: .... Notary Public

SEAL-STAMP   NORTH CAROLINA, COUNTY OF ....

Use Black Ink

I, ..., a Notary Public of the County and State aforesaid,

certify that ...., personally came before me this day and acknowledged

that ...... he is .... Secretary of .... a North

Carolina corporation, and that by authority duly given and as the act of the corporation, the foregoing instrument

was signed in its name by its .... President, sealed with its corporate seal and attested by ....

as its ....Secretary.

Witness my hand and official stamp or seal, this ....day of ...., 19.........

My commission expires: .... Notary Public

The foregoing Certificate(s) of ....

....

....

is/are certified to be correct. This instrument and this certificate are duly registered at the date and time and in the Book and Page shown on the first page hereof.

....REGISTER OF DEEDS FOR...COUNTY

By ....Deputy/Assistant - Register of Deeds

N.C. Bar Assoc. Form No. 3 © 1976

There is a type of deed which makes no warranties whatsoever. It is called a *quitclaim deed,* and simply conveys whatever rights and interests (if any) the grantor may have. This deed is commonly used to clear up clouds on title. For example, if there is a possibility that X might have some claim that he could later assert against the property, X would be asked to execute a quitclaim deed to this property, simply to avoid a potential dispute, and to make the present state of the title free of clouds and therefore "clear and marketable."

One of the important components of the deed is the description of the property. This should be accurate enough so that the particular property can be identified as to exact location, boundaries, etc.

Probably the most common form of property description is by *metes and bounds.* Metes are measurements of distance; bounds are boundaries, both natural and artificial (streams, streets, etc.).

The following illustration may be helpful:

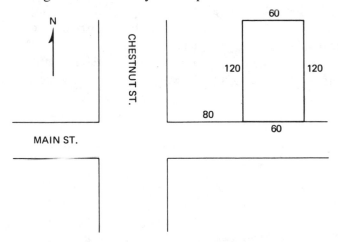

A description of this property might read:

Beginning at a point on the northerly side of Main Street distant 80 feet easterly, from the corner formed by the intersection of the northerly side of Main St. with the easterly side of Chestnut Street, running thence northerly and parallel with Chestnut St. 120 feet; running thence easterly and parallel with Main St. 60 feet; running thence southerly and parallel with Chestnut St. 120 feet to the northerly side of Main St.; running thence westerly along the northerly side of Main St. 60 feet to the point or place of beginning.

Note that there is a "point of beginning," an exact starting place to which we must return in order to "close" the figure reflecting the shape of the property.

Sometimes, in the case of a property located in a residential sub-division or "development," where the plan of the entire tract has been recorded, a description of the property might simply read "lot number 11 of the Happy Acres sub-division." The exact measurements and directions of the lot can be seen in the recorded map of the development (called a "plat") filed in the appropriate office, such as the Register of Deeds. Whatever the plat shows lot number 11 to be would be the shape and dimensions of the lot.

Another system for the property description is called the *rectangular* or *government survey* system. This is a standardized system established by the U.S. Government almost 200 years ago, and is used in many parts of the country, with the exception of Texas and the states along the eastern coastline.

This system is based on a grid of surveying lines—both east-west and north-south—that are standard, and are used to establish quadrangles. These are further sub-divided into *townships* (not to be confused with the local governmental "townships"). Each township is 36 square miles and is further divided into 36 sections of 1 square mile each. These sections are numbered in a standard pattern for ready identification.

The following illustration of a township shows the numbered sections it contains:

6	5	4	3	2	1
7	8	9	10	11	12
18	17	16	15	14	13
19	20	21	22	23	24
30	29	28	27	26	25
31	32	33	34	35	36

Since each section is 1 mile square, it contains 640 acres. A particular parcel may be described, for example, as "The Northwest ¼ of section

21.'' Let us illustrate how this would be computed by taking section 21 and quartering it:

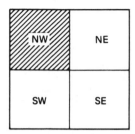

Since the total area of the section is 640 acres, the N.W. one-fourth must be 160 acres.

If the description were ''The Northwest ¼ of the Southeast ¼,'' we would do the same by quartering first the entire section (to establish the Southeast one-fourth) and then quartering *that* one-fourth to establish *its* Northwest one-fourth:

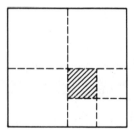

In determining the acreage of any particular property under the rectangular system, the key lies in starting with the *last* portion described, and working backward; what we are doing is starting with the largest segment, and subdividing as we work backward.

To illustrate, let us find the ''Northwest ¼ of the Northeast ¼ of the Southwest ¼.'' We start by marking off the last item (Southwest ¼); we then quarter this and mark off the next item (going backward), the Northeast ¼; we then mark off the Northwest ¼.

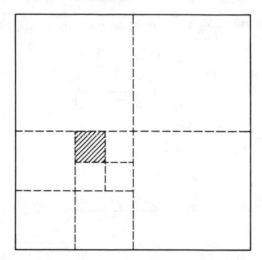

In this example, our parcel would comprise 10 acres. (¼ of ¼ of ¼ of 640 acres.)

Obviously this system would be unwieldy in urban areas, where typical residential lots are small in size. In most such areas, local mapping has produced a system of numbered sections, containing numbered blocks, each of which in turn consists of specific numbered lots. Thus, in a city such as New York, a particular lot might be identified as "section 408, block 1157, lot 32."

Wills and Descent

Title to real property may also be transferred from an owner who has died. This is true not only where a will has been left, but also where the deceased has left no will.

One who makes a will is called a *testator,* and he is said to have died *testate*. One who dies leaving no will is said to have died *intestate.*

Usually any interest in land that can be transferred during one's lifetime may be validly transferred by will. This assumes, of course, that the will complies with the particular state's requirements for a valid will.

Since a will is an instrument designed to take effect only upon the testator's death, it is of no legal effect prior to that time. If Smith makes a will leaving real property to Jones, Jones has no legal interest in that property while Smith is alive. Smith has the right to change or revoke the will at any time.

A gift of real property by will is called a *devise,* and the recipient of the gift is therefore a *devisee.* In his will, the testator nominates an *executor* who, with the approval of the court, is empowered to carry out the provisions of the will.

In the situation where a deceased dies *intestate,* title to his property passes to heirs according to the statutes of the particular state. Usually such statutes distribute the property according to the degree of closeness of the surviving relatives. In such case, instead of an executor, there is an *administrator* appointed by the court to settle the affairs of the estate.

Suppose a deceased leaves no will and no surviving relatives can be found? In this relatively rare situation, his property goes to the state by what is called *escheat.* The justification for this is that land is too valuable a commodity to be "unowned," therefore economically unproductive.

Eminent Domain

This is the basic right of a sovereign government to take private property for some public use.

Since, as we saw earlier, private ownership of real property is always subject to this governmental right, eminent domain can bring about a situation where title to property is transferred not by voluntary act of the owner, but involuntarily.

In this situation, government acquires title by a legal proceeding called *condemnation.* The owner must be paid a fair compensation for the property taken.

For property to be taken under the right of eminent domain, it must be necessary for the public use specified. This does not mean that a road, for example, could not be built differently. The requirement is simply that the road to be built as specified requires the taking of the property in question.

The compensation to be paid to the property owner really amounts to indemnifying him for the loss suffered as a result of the taking, and this theory is well-established by many court decisions. But suppose A and B are adjoining property owners, and only A's property is taken in condemnation proceedings. If B's property suffers a loss in value because of the taking, B is not entitled to any award, since he has no interest in the property taken.

Interestingly enough, if a business is being conducted on the property taken, no additional compensation is paid for loss of business. This is the general rule, and is justified on the ground that the profits of a business enterprise arise not from the land but from the owner's investment of capital and labor.

The mechanics of the condemnation proceeding, by which the governmental authority acquires title to the property, and the award to the property owner is confirmed, are not uniform. They vary from state to state, and those interested in pursuing further study of condemnation proceedings under the right of eminent domain should refer to the particular statutes of their respective states.

Adverse Possession

This is an interesting theory by which it is possible for one who possesses and uses property to acquire good title to it. In effect, the law is penalizing an owner who fails to protect his interest.

Statutes vary from state to state, but they usually require that the occupant maintain a continuous possession, "open and notorious," hostile to the record owner, for a specified number of years. In North Carolina, for example, this period is 20 years (which is the most common required period), but if the occupancy is under "color of title" (some instrument which purports to give title, even though ultimately shown to be defective), the required period is only 7 years.

Some states also provide for such acquisition of title if the real property taxes are paid over a specified number of years by the claimant in possession.

There are some basic requirements for the doctrine of adverse possession to apply. For one, there must be actual possession of the property. This is demonstrated not only by the intention to occupy the land, but by some physical act evidencing this intention (cultivating the land, building on it, etc.).

The possession must also be "open and notorious," which means that the acts of possession must be such that they are apparent to outside eyes. This requirement becomes obvious when you consider the basis for the entire theory of adverse possession—if the purpose is to penalize an owner who fails to take action to protect his interest, how could this logically be justified if he had no way of knowing that such interest was being jeopardized?

The possession must also be exclusive with the claimant. There can be no "exclusive possession" if there are a number of claimants occupying the land at the same time.

Another requirement is that the possession be *continuous* for the period required. While this might not require physical presence on the land each and every day, it would require that the reasonable use of the land must be uninterrupted. For example, land whose use consists of seasonal cultivation could reasonably be said to be in continuous possession if the claimant engaged in this activity each season.

An interesting sidelight to this requirement of continuity exists in the case where a claimant transfers his interest to another, perhaps by deed or will. (This is not without legal justification; after all, a claimant, during the period of his occupancy, does have property rights against anyone except the true owner). If claimant A, after being in possession for 11 years, transfers his interest to B, who takes immediate possession and uses the property continuously for 9 more years, this would satisfy a 20 year statutory requirement. Courts generally have recognized the principle of "tacking," by which B's period is tacked onto A's.

What sort of title is acquired by a claimant who satisfies the statutory requirements we have outlined? The answer is that he acquires title that is good not only against the owner of record, but against all the world as well. It is as valid a title as though he had acquired it by a deed of transfer from the owner.

Would this title be acceptable to a prospective purchaser? The answer is debatable. We shall see later that a purchaser generally is entitled to what is called "marketable" title, and while the claimant under adverse possession may have complied with the statutory requirements, his title is based upon matters not of record. One way of solidifying his position would be for the claimant to take legal action asking for some sort of "declaratory judgment"—a court decree declaring him to be the owner, presumably giving him the right to record this, thus becoming the owner "of record."

. The frequency of present-day applications of the doctrine of adverse possession is not great. It arises perhaps most often in situations involving encroachments, probably through mistake as to the exact location of a property line. For example, if a structure or fence extends over one's property line, and the adjoining property owner takes no corrective action within the statutory period provided for, the encroaching owner may be considered to have acquired title to that portion of the land encroached upon.

LAND USE CONTROL

As we mentioned, ownership of land may carry limitations on the use of the land, and these limitations may be either privately or governmentally imposed.

As to those privately imposed, the law allows any property owner to impose restrictions on the use of property he transfers, so long as those restrictions do not violate any law, and are not against public policy (such as racial restrictions). The most frequently encountered restrictions are those involving residential subdivisions, where the developer wishes to maintain a particular level of attractiveness and marketability in the area. There may be minimum dwelling area requirements, a maximum number of families specified per dwelling unit, prohibition of commercial enterprises, a requirement that dwellings be set back a certain number of feet from the roadway, and similar restrictions.

When a deed contains specific promises (covenants) to refrain from using land in a certain way, these promises are called *restrictive covenants*. In a sense they are "negative covenants" in that they are promises *not* to do certain things. In the typical case of the residential subdivision, the deed to an individual lot buyer need not list all of the restrictions; usually those restrictions have been recorded in the office of the Register of Deeds, or other appropriate office, and the deed may simply recite the fact that the transfer is made subject to those recorded restrictions. The grantee would then be bound by those restrictions, since they are on record, and therefore open to inspection.

Restrictive covenants generally "run with the land" meaning that they "go with" the land, so that a subsequent purchaser is bound by the restrictions, so long as they have been recorded, even though he may be unaware of their existence. Another illustration of the importance of a title search!

Where a restrictive covenant is violated, enforcement may be sought even by one who was not a party to the property transfer. In a development, for example, since the restrictive covenants were imposed for the benefit of all property holders in the development, a property owner who violates any of the restrictions may find himself subject to legal action by any one or more of the other property owners in the development.

Great care should be taken in choosing the language of a restriction. Suppose it states that "no structure shall be erected other than a dwelling." If the purchaser of land builds a home, and later conducts a business therein (a barber shop, perhaps), can he be said to have violated the restriction? Probably not, since the requirement was only that the structure *erected* be a dwelling. A better choice of language would have been to prohibit the "use" of any lot for any purpose other than as a dwelling.

Residential subdivisions often include a requirement that no structure may be erected unless the plans and specifications have first been approved by the owner of the subdivision. Presumably this is done to assure that new homes will be of such design and quality of construction as not to affect adversely the appearance of the area and the market value of other homes in the development. While the requirement for such approval is valid and enforceable, it must be applied reasonably. If, for example, the owner of the development arbitrarily and unreasonably withholds his approval—in an attempt, perhaps, to prevent a particular lot buyer from becoming a resident of the area—the courts will not enforce the provision.

Turning to public or governmental control of land use, we find that *zoning* is the chief method by which government attempts to implement some sort of "master plan" of orderly growth. By establishing zones, with particular requirements and restrictions within each type of zone, government may control such matters as land use, height and size of buildings, density of population, etc. Land use districts are generally divided into broad categories such as residential, commercial and industrial; these may be further subdivided so that under "residential" we might find classifications such as one-family, multi-family, apartment houses, and others.

The right of municipalities and counties to establish and enforce zoning regulations derives from the state under the latter's "police power," a term used to describe that power the state has to act in the interest of the well-being of its citizens—their general welfare, health and safety.

When zoning regulations are enacted, they cannot affect an existing structure or use, since this would be obviously unfair. Such a use is called a *non-conforming use,* and is protected so long as that use is continuous.

To illustrate, suppose a zoning regulation is enacted prohibiting commercial establishments in a certain area. Smith has been operating a dry cleaning establishment in the area for the past three years, and will therefore be allowed to continue operation as a "non-conforming" use. In fact, most ordinances permit one who buys Smith's establishment to continue operating the business, so long as he does not expand or change the use. Whether a rebuilding of the operation would be permitted after destruction, such as by fire, depends on the particular local zoning ordinance. Most ordinances prohibit the re-establishment of the non-conforming use if such use has been discontinued for a specified period of time.

In special circumstances, perhaps involving hardship, a property owner may ask for a *variance,* special permission to use his property in a manner prohibited by the zoning regulation. It is important to distinguish this from a request for a change in zoning, which involves a request to re-zone an area from one classification to another. The granting of a variance does not alter the existing zoning classification in any way.

Requests for variances, as well as re-zoning petitions, would normally be presented to the local zoning board.

Sometimes a particular tract may be "spot zoned" for some use different from that for which the general area is zoned. An example might be a shopping center within an area zoned for residential use.

Generally, churches and public schools are not subject to zoning ordinances, and so cannot be excluded from residential areas. Whether private schools enjoy this privilege is debatable, since court decisions have not been uniform in their holdings; the predominant view, however, is that private schools, like public schools, cannot be excluded.

Most of us think of zoning as an exclusionary device designed to keep business and industry out of residential areas. While zoning is exclusionary, it can be used to exclude residences from areas designed to be reserved for business. If a community is to encourage business and industry, it may need to assure that residential building growth will not swallow up areas needed for commercial activity. As we mentioned earlier, the supply of land is limited, and that fact dictates the necessity for a far-sighted planning of land use.

It should be pointed out that some recent court decisions have affected zoning provisions in a manner quite unanticipated. Various legal actions have been brought attacking the validity of such regulations as minimum lot size requirements in suburban communities, on the ground that such requirements, since they exclude a *class* (the less-affluent), are unconstitutional. Some courts have supported this view, the theory being that zoning should be for the benefit of all citizens, and that to deprive those of lower economic level from access to land (by virtue of minimum lot sizes they cannot afford) is unfairly discriminatory.

It would probably be accurate to describe this trend as an outgrowth of the impact of civil-rights awareness and the recognition of claims on behalf of minorities. Since such groups contain a disproportionately large number of economically "disadvantaged," courts have leaned toward the theory that much local zoning—particularly the large-lot requirement—is used as a device by which to exclude members of minority groups from becoming residents of the community.

OPEN HOUSING

No discussion of limitations on a property owner's rights would be complete without reference to legislation and court decisions prohibiting unfair discrimination in the transfer of any interest in property. The emphasis on "civil rights" in recent years has made it particularly important for the real estate industry to be aware of the penalties involved—possibly criminal as well as civil—in not selling or leasing property to an individual because of his or her race, color, religion, or national origin.

After the Civil War, Congress passed the Civil Rights Act of 1866, providing that "all citizens of the United States shall have the same right, in every State and Territory, as is enjoyed by white citizens thereof to inherit, purchase, lease, sell, hold, and convey real and personal property."

Almost 100 years later, in 1965, a Negro named Jones brought suit against a St. Louis developer, alleging that he had been refused a home because of his color, and claiming that such refusal constituted a violation of the 1866 legislation. The case was dismissed by the court, and Jones appealed the decision. The appeal court upheld the decision, and Jones then appealed to the U.S. Supreme Court which in 1968 reversed the lower court's decision, holding that the developer's conduct violated the 1866 Act. The court further stated that the act barred all racial discrimination, public and private, and that the act was constitutional as a valid exercise of the power of Congress to enforce the thirteenth amendment to the U.S. Constitution.

Meanwhile, in 1968, Congress passed the Fair Housing Act of 1968 which made it illegal, in a rental or sale, to discriminate on the basis of race, color, religion, or national origin. This legislation carried certain exemptions, such as the property owner who sells his home without the services of a broker. However, the Supreme Court decision in the Jones case invalidates such exemptions, and effectively broadens the scope of the 1866 Civil Rights Act.

Additionally, the Fair Housing Act prohibits certain activities such as discriminatory advertising and making false statements concerning the availability of housing for sale or rent. It also prohibits certain activity commonly referred to as "blockbusting"—the use of scare tactics to induce property owners to sell their homes by telling the owners that members of minority groups are moving into the neighborhood.

To summarize, the prohibition against *any* unfair discrimination, in *any* transaction, is a result of a combination of three events, each of which either supplements or overlaps another:

1. The Civil Rights Act of 1866
2. The Jones decision of the Supreme Court
3. The Fair Housing Act of 1968

It is therefore wise for anyone, whether licensed real estate professional or property owner, to be fully aware of the broad application of the anti-discrimination law, and to avoid any activity that might come within its prohibitions.

2.

THE BROKER'S ROLE AND FUNCTION

To understand the legal status of the real estate broker, we must know something about the law of agency. Generally, an individual (called a principal) may designate someone else (called an *agent*) to represent him in dealing with a third party.

In real estate, the principal is the property owner who wishes to sell. He contracts with the broker (the agent) to deal with a third party (the potential buyer). While it is possible for a broker to represent a buyer rather than a seller, this is not the typical situation.

The law of agency recognizes variations in the scope of an agent's authority. A real estate broker has a rather limited authority, since he usually does not have the right to execute binding agreements on behalf of his principal. His job is simply to procure a purchaser ready, willing, and able to purchase his principal's property, either at the listed price or at some other price agreed to by the seller.

A broker is a *fiduciary*, a term used to describe one who occupies a position of trust, in which the highest duty of loyalty and good faith is imposed. He is therefore under certain obligations to his principal. For example, since he owes his principal the duty of loyalty, he cannot act for both parties in a transaction, unless they both are aware of that fact.

He cannot profit from his relationship by collecting some secret fee, or by using information unknown to his principal. In fact, he is under a duty to disclose to the principal any information pertinent to the subject of his agency.

For example, suppose there is a substantial increase in the value of the property during the time the broker has the listing and is attempting to find a buyer. The broker's failure to disclose this fact could constitute a violation of his fiduciary obligation. Similarly, the broker must disclose to his principal anything he knows about a prospective buyer (perhaps a doubtful financial condition; or even the fact that he is related to the broker). In other words, he must advise the seller of any information he has which might reasonably be expected to influence the seller's action in selling his property.

As part of his obligation of loyalty to his principal, a broker cannot act for both sides in a transaction, but if both sides are aware that he is acting thus, then he is not in violation. In this situation, therefore, the broker is under a duty to advise each party of his "dual agency."

The broker also must exercise that degree of skill and care ordinarily expected of one in his profession, and his failure along these lines could subject him to legal action for damages.

This has become particularly significant recently with the enormous increase in lawsuits against professionals in all fields. Along with "consumer protection" has come an overawareness of litigation and the readiness of purchasers of goods or services to bring suit if they believe there is the slightest likelihood of receiving any compensation.

The broker must also maintain records, and is financially accountable to his principal, for any money received on the principal's behalf. He is prohibited from "commingling" (mixing) his personal funds with money belonging to his principal. In North Carolina, for example, the law requires that he maintain a special account in an insured bank or savings and loan association within the state, and all money received by the broker on behalf of a principal is to be deposited in this account.

The requirement of such escrow account for moneys of clients is found in almost every state.

What about misrepresentations made by a broker in his attempt to sell property? Of course, if a broker makes such statements on his own, he is liable to the buyer. But such a situation might even make the broker liable ultimately to his principal. For example, if the broker's misrepresentations induced the buyer to consummate the purchase, and upon later learning of the deception, the buyer sued the seller and was awarded damages, (since the seller is generally liable for the acts of his agent), the seller could recover from the broker. The legal justification for such recovery would rest on the fact that the broker, in making the representations—thus subjecting his principal to potential liability—had violated his duty to his principal.

A breach of duty by a broker carries three possible consequences:

1. Revocation or suspension of his license by the state real estate board.
2. Liability in a lawsuit for damages.
3. Criminal liability if the broker's conduct constituted a crime. In

North Carolina, violation of the licensing law is a misdemeanor; if the conduct complained of constitutes a more serious offense (embezzlement, fraud, etc.) the broker could be charged with a felony.

How does the agency relationship between broker and client arise in the first place? For this relationship to be created there must be a contract of employment by which the broker's services are being engaged. (Do not be misled by the word "employment;" the broker is not an employee, but an agent). The agreement under which he will operate is called a *listing contract* or agreement.

In any dispute over brokerage commission, should a legal action be necessary, the basic requirement to establish a claim is the existence of an employment agreement. Without proof that the broker was engaged by the principal, no suit will be entertained by the court. Therefore, as in the case of any contractual agreement, it is best to have this agreement in writing. Although many states recognize the validity of an oral listing agreement, the difficulty of proof, and the probability of honest misunderstanding, make it highly undesirable. In North Carolina, a written listing agreement cannot be for an indefinite period; it must provide for a definite expiration date, at which time it will expire, unless the parties agree to a continuation.

Let us define the various types of listing agreements:

Exclusive right to sell

Here the broker is given the sole and exclusive right to sell the property, so that if he *or anyone* sells it, the broker is entitled to the commission. The broker receives the commission even if the owner himself sells the property.

What if the property is bought, after the expiration of the listing agreement, by one to whom the property had been shown by the broker? For the broker's protection, the listing agreement usually specifies a time period (perhaps 3 or 4 months) after the termination of the agreement during which the broker would still be entitled to commission if the property is bought by one to whom he had shown it during the listing period.

Exclusive agency

Here the broker is the only agency empowered to sell the property but the owner retains the right to sell it himself without being liable for commission. Should the owner effect such a sale, the listing agreement is automatically terminated.

Open listing

The property is listed with any number of brokers, each of whom—as well as the owner—has the right to sell. The sale by any one automatically terminates the listing agreements of the others.

Multiple listing

Here the brokers in a particular area form a membership group by which members may sell property originally listed by other members.

The listing agreement provides for putting the property on this multiple listing service, and the property description and photographs are then circulated to the other members. If the property is sold by a broker other than the listing broker, the commission is divided between the listing and selling brokers. Since the law prohibits "standardized" fees or commissions, the split of commission is negotiable, but usually follows a pattern, often a straight 50-50 division.

The multiple listing bureau usually gets either a small percentage of the commissions, or a flat fee of perhaps $10 or $15 for each property listed. In some areas, broker members pay a monthly membership fee.

For the seller of property, the multiple listing gives him greater exposure by having all the broker members show the property. For a prospective buyer, it eliminates the necessity for having various brokers show him properties; by contacting just one broker, he can see all the properties so listed.

A typical multiple listing agreement is shown on the following page.

Net listing

While legal and valid in most states, this type of listing is generally frowned upon. In it, the seller establishes a "net" amount he wishes to receive, and anything over that amount is to be the broker's commission.

The likelihood of dispute is great, and the loss of commission quite possible. For example, if the broker receives an offer of an amount equal to the net desired by the seller, he is under a duty to communicate the offer. Should it be accepted by the seller, the broker would have earned nothing for his efforts.

On the other hand, if the broker finds a buyer at a price substantially

Exclusive Listing Contract

BURKE COUNTY MULTIPLE LISTING SERVICE
Morganton, North Carolina

In consideration of your agreement to list the following property for sale and to use your efforts to find a purchaser, the undersigned seller (for identification, hereinafter referred to as the seller, whether one or more) agrees with you, as our Listing Agent, as follows:

1. *Exclusive Right to Sell.* You shall have the exclusive right to sell the property as our Listing Agent at the price and on the terms set forth below or such other price that we may agree upon, until midnight.., 19..............

2. *Property to be Sold.*...

3. *Sale price* $..

4. *Terms of Sale*:   1—Cash (   )   2—L.A. (   )   3—Conv. (   )   4—FHA (   )   5—VA (   )   6—Personal (   )

5. *Multiple Listing.* This listing shall be (   ) shall not be (   ) entered in the Burke County Multiple Listing Service.

6. *Cooperation with Agent.* Seller agrees to cooperate with you (or other agent acting for or through you) to facilitate the sale of the property. Property may be shown only by appointment made by or through you as Listing Agent.

7. *Commission.* Seller agrees to pay you a commission if a purchaser is procured by you, the Seller, or anyone else during the exclusive listing period. Commission to be..............................% and shall be computed on the gross sales price of the property.

8. *Later Sale to Prospect.* Such compensation shall be paid if property is sold, conveyed or otherwise transferred within .... days after the termination of this authority or any extension thereof to anyone with whom agent has had negotiations prior to final termination, provided I have received notice in writing, including the names of the prospective purchasers, before or upon termination of this agreement or any extension thereof. However, I shall not be obligated to pay such compensation if a valid listing agreement is entered into during the term of said protection period with another licensed real estate broker and a sale, lease or exchange of the property is made during the term of said protection period.

9. *Title to be Conveyed.* Seller acknowledges right of ownership of the property and agrees that a deed will be executed and delivered to a purchaser conveying an indefeasible fee simple title to the property with full warranties subject only to such easements and restrictions as appear of record.

10. *Possession.* Seller agrees to give a purchaser possession of the property ....

11. *For Sale Sign.* You may place a "For Sale" sign on the property: Yes:.............. No:.............. Seller agrees to remove all other signs.

12. *The property which is the subject matter of this agreement, and as herein before described, is offered without respect to race, creed, color, or national origin.*

13. *Other Special Provisions.* ....

Agreed to and accepted this..............day of..........................., 19..............   ....(Seal)
                                                                                            Seller (or other)

                                                                                                              ....(Seal)
....
(Listing Agent Firm)   Seller

                                                                            Address: ....

                              (Seal)   Zip
....   Code.........................
(Firm Representative)   ....

                                                                            Phone: Home.......................... Office..........................

Address.. Zoned.................. Price $.................. MLS No..........................

Section.. Miles from Center City.............. Lot Size..............................

Type Exterior.................................. Furnished ( ) Unfurnished ( ) Frontage..........................

Floors	Main	2nd	Lower	GENERAL INFORMATION		
Ent. Hall				Stove/Oven	Laundry	Cond. In
Liv. Room				Ref. ( ) D.W. ( ) Disp. ( )	Water Source	Cond. Out
Din. Room				Vent Hood	Sewerage	School Elem.
Kitchen				ATTIC (Size)	Roof Cond. Mat.	School Jr.
Brk. Room				Stairs	Carpet	School Sr.
Den				Fan	Drapes	Real Tax Value
Recreation				BASEMENT	Insulated	Type Loan
Bedrooms				Size	Storm Windows	Held By
Baths				Floor	Storm Doors	Amt. Due
Closets				In/Out Ent.	CP/Gar.	Int. Rate
Floors				Heat	Drive	Payments
Walls				Fireplaces	Porch Patio	Includes
Utility Rm.				Air Cond.	In or Out of City.	DB P
Sq. Ft. Htd.				Water Heater	Age	Tax Id. No.

Average Utility Costs

Remarks:

Road No. and Name .... State Maintained: Yes ( ) No ( )   Paved: Yes ( ) No ( )

Directions:

Owner's Name .... Phone No...................... Is Property Occupied?...............

Listing Agent (Firm) .... Phone No.............. Listing Salesman.............................. Phone No...............

Possession .... Make Appointments Through .... Key At ....

The information shown herein is furnished by the owner according to the best of his knowledge and belief but is subject to verification by the purchaser, and the agent assumes no responsibility for the correctness thereof.

F-1   Rev. 8/15/78

above the seller's net, he is perhaps vulnerable to the charge that he misled the seller by not disclosing that the property was worth a good deal more than the seller believed it was.

Listing agreements in any given area have become fairly well standardized. Some of the important components would be: (1) price of the property and terms of the sale; (2) description of the property; (3) the amount of commission; (4) date of expiration of the listing; (5) signatures of the parties.

The basic purpose of a listing agreement is to employ the services of a broker in finding a purchaser. But there are situations where a prospective purchaser cannot make an immediate decision, yet does not wish to lose the opportunity to buy. He might be willing to pay for an *option,* which is the right to purchase the property for a specified price within a specified time period. An option is nothing more than a promise by the seller not to sell to anyone else until the prospective purchaser has made his decision.

An option is a type of contract. Therefore there must be *consideration* paid for the seller's promise to hold the property open. A mere promise by the seller to give the prospective buyer time to decide, without any payment by the buyer, is not enforceable. Also, the option agreement must be in writing.

Often the parties agree that if the prospective buyer decides to buy, the amount he paid for the option will be applied toward the purchase price of the property. If the decision is not to buy, there is no further obligation, and the amount paid for the option is retained by the seller.

We mentioned earlier that a broker's function is to find a purchaser ready, willing and able to buy, either on the terms of the listing agreement or upon such terms as are accepted by the seller. When, then, has a broker earned his commission? Generally, it is held that the broker is entitled to his commission by having produced this buyer, so that even if the seller or buyer later changes his mind and refuses to consummate the transaction, the broker may still recover his commission.

The term "ready, willing and able" has significance. The buyer might be ready and willing, but not financially "able." As we shall see in discussing offers to purchase, unless the buyer expects to pay all cash for the property (not a typical occurrence) the agreement between the parties usually provides that the deal is conditioned upon the buyer's ability to obtain a mortgage loan. The broker's commission will therefore not be earned unless and until the buyer is able to obtain such a loan.

The seller and broker might agree that commission is to be paid only if the transaction is completed and title actually passes from seller to buyer;

in such case, the broker would not be entitled to commission unless that event takes place.

Aside from these special arrangements, however, listing agreements generally contain such language as "seller agrees to pay you a commission if a purchaser is procured by you," and the broker would therefore have earned his commission when he produced a buyer ready, willing and able who either offered what the seller had asked or made a different offer which the seller thereafter accepted.

Suppose a broker shows a property to a prospect who later contacts the owners himself, and a deal is consummated without the broker's assistance. Is the broker entitled to his commission? He is, under the general rule that commission is earned if the broker was the *procuring cause* of the sale.

The phrase *"procuring cause"* is usually defined in terms of a broker's actions which, by a connected series of events, bring about the consummation of the transaction. But this is not always easily applied, particularly in a case where two brokers are claiming the commission.

Suppose broker A originally introduced a prospective buyer to the seller, and this prospect later concluded the deal through broker B. Which broker was the procuring cause? A decision would have to depend on the particular facts—did broker A abandon his efforts? Or, to paraphrase a familiar case, did broker B simply step in and pick up the fruit after A had shaken the tree?

The contract of sale between seller and buyer usually contains a statement by which the parties acknowledge that a particular broker effected the deal. But of course, another broker is free to pursue a legal remedy if he feels that the commission should be his.

With regard to deposit money received by the broker, this deposit belongs to the seller, and the broker ordinarily would be required to turn it over promptly if the deposit is forfeited by reason of the buyer's failure to go through with the deal. But since the broker did what he was engaged to do (find a purchaser) he is entitled to his commission. The contract of sale usually provides that if the buyer breaches the contract (by failing to go through with the deal) the deposit is forfeited, and becomes the property of the broker, to be credited toward the commission due him. Of course, if the amount of the deposit exceeds the commission, the difference would be returned to the seller.

The broker's agency terminates when a buyer is found. If either the seller or the broker dies, that too will terminate the agency.

Does an owner have the right to terminate the agency before its expiration date? The answer points out the interesting distinction between the *power* to do an act and the legal *right* to do it. If Mr. Seller gives Mr. Broker a 90-day listing agreement, Seller can effectively terminate the agency during the 90-day period, and the broker can no longer act on behalf of seller—BUT seller may be liable for commission if broker has already produced a buyer. Furthermore, if broker is in the midst of negotiations with a prospective buyer, seller might be liable to broker for damages, since seller's act was a breach of his agreement with broker.

In other words, seller has the *power* to terminate the agency at any time; but he does not have the *right* to break his agreement by termination before the expiration date.

A final word before we leave the subject of broker's function. We have stressed the broker's duties to his principal, the seller; but this does not mean that he is under no obligation to the prospective buyer he produces. He has a duty not to make any false representations or engage in any conduct that is fraudulent. He may make general statements considered to be "puffing," or "sales talk," but he may become liable to the buyer if he makes a factual statement (for example, "This house has no termites") that is false. A knowledgeable broker never makes representations about the property unless those statements of fact come from the seller, so that they are the seller's representations. Even then, a broker is under a duty to check for himself those things that are verifiable. In one case, a broker had "fireplace" listed as one of the features of the house he was selling. The buyer, on the first night of his occupancy, after taking title, lit a fire in the fireplace and discovered—by way of heavy soot and smoke damage—that the "fireplace" was one in appearance only; it had no flue. The broker was held liable for the damage.

3.

THE CONTRACT OF SALE

All of us, at one time or another, have bought or sold some article of personal property—a wristwatch, let us say. The transaction was decided on and consummated simultaneously; the buyer handed over the money, the seller transferred the watch, and the deal was over, nothing remaining to be done.

Such is not typically the case with real property. Much must be done between the time that the parties agree on the deal and the actual transfer of title, not the least of which is a careful search of the records (title search) to make sure that the title to be transferred is free of any possible claims by others.

Since the length of time between the agreement of sale and the actual "title closing" (transfer of title) may run from a few weeks to a few months, it is important that there be a binding, enforceable contract during this period, so that both buyer and seller will feel secure. We will now consider how this contract comes about.

A contract, by definition, is any agreement that is valid and enforceable at law. For an agreement to fall into this category, certain essentials are required.

1. There must be a valid offer and acceptance.
2. Consideration must be present.
3. The parties must be legally competent (not insane, under age, etc.).
4. The object or purpose of the agreement must not be illegal.
5. Certain types of contracts must be in writing (such as those transferring an interest in real property).

The technicalities of these essentials are beyond the scope of this book, but we should be aware of the basic requirements of any valid contract.

When a purchaser is ready to make an offer, the broker will have him execute an *offer to purchase*. This is a document by which the prospective purchaser indicates the price and terms under which he is willing to buy.

He accompanies the execution of this document with a deposit, and it is then the broker's duty to convey this instrument to his principal, the seller. If the seller agrees to the terms and conditions, he too signs it, and it then becomes a binding agreement.

In some areas, a simple "receipt of deposit" form is used, with the intention of having the parties later execute a more detailed and formal "contract of sale." However, even in such cases buyer and seller should be aware that if the basic information is set forth, the signatures of buyer and seller, together with the acceptance of the deposit, create a binding agreement.

In many areas, it is customary to use one form as an "offer to purchase and contract for sale of real estate." In such cases it is not necessary to execute any further contract, since all of the details are included in this form. The basic elements in such a contract are the following:

1. Acknowledge receipt of the deposit.
2. Description of the property.
3. Agreement to sell and agreement to buy at specified price and terms.
4. States any conditions of purchase (such as making the transaction conditioned on buyer being able to arrange a mortgage loan).
5. States the type of deed to be given and the place and date of closing title.

A typical "offer to purchase and contract" is shown on the following page.

These are basic, but other provisions are necessary in order to avoid any misunderstanding or dispute between the parties. Some of these are the following:

1. Disposition of the deposit ("earnest money") in the event of a breach of the contract.
2. Requirement that appliances, electrical and heating components, etc. be in good working order at time of title closing.
3. Provision for termite inspection.

A deposit is not a legal requirement for an offer to purchase (or contract of sale) to be valid. But you can readily see why it is most desirable, and why it is the usual practice to require one.

Let us assume that Mr. Byers and Mr. Sellers have signed their contract of sale. Who is now the owner of the property? Your answer should be unhesitating; Mr. Sellers is still the owner because title has not yet passed, and will not pass until "title closing" date. But there is a contractual obligation here; Mr. Sellers is obligating himself to transfer

OFFER TO PURCHASE AND CONTRACT

Buyer ....

Mailing Address .... Phone No. ....

Seller ....

Mailing Address .... Phone No. ....

Realtor ....

Mailing Address .... Phone No. ....

Real Property ....

....

Personal Property ....

....

Buyer hereby offers to purchase the real and personal property above described from Seller in accordance with the Standard Provisions on the **Reverse Side Hereof** and the following terms and conditions; upon acceptance of this offer, this shall become a contract binding upon the parties:

1. PURCHASE PRICE: The purchase price is $... and shall be paid as follows:

(a) $..........................., by assumption of the unpaid principal balance and all obligations of Seller on the existing loan secured by a deed of trust on the above described property.

(b) $..........................., by a promissory note secured by a purchase money deed of trust on the property with interest prior to default at the rate of ....% per annum, payable by .... payments of $..........................., commencing on .... Prepayment rights, if any, shall be: ....

....

Buyer's right to convey subject to or with assumption, if any, shall be: ....

....

(c) $..........................., the balance of the purchase price in cash at closing.

2. EARNEST MONEY: The sum of $........................... in earnest money is hereby deposited in escrow with: .... to guarantee the faithful performance by Buyer hereunder and to be applied on the purchase price at closing.

3. CONDITIONS: [State N/A in each blank of paragraph 3(a) and 3(b) that is not a condition to this contract]

(a) The Buyer must be able upon the exercise of due diligence to obtain a firm commitment acceptable to Buyer for a loan in the principal amount of $........................... for a term of .... years, at an interest rate not to exceed ....% prior to .... Buyer agrees to advise Seller immediately upon his acceptance of such firm commitment.

(b) There must be no restriction, easement, zoning or other governmental regulation that would prevent the reasonable use of the real property for .... purposes.

4. OTHER PROVISIONS AND CONDITIONS:

(a) All of the Standard Provisions on the **Reverse Side Hereof** are understood and shall apply to this instrument, except the following numbered Standard Provisions shall be deleted: ....
(If none are to be deleted, state "None" in this blank)

5. CLOSING: All parties agree to execute any and all documents and papers necessary in connection with closing and transfer of title on or before ...., at a place designated by .... Deed is to be made to ....

6. POSSESSION: Possession shall be delivered ....; in the event that Buyer has agreed that possession is not delivered at closing, then Seller agrees to pay to Buyer the sum of .... per day to and including the date that possession is to be delivered as above set forth.

7. COUNTERPARTS: This Offer and Contract is executed in .... counterparts with an executed counterpart being retained by each party hereto.

Date of Offer: .... Date of Acceptance: ....

....[Seal] ....[Seal]
Buyer   Seller (Owner)

....[Seal] ....[Seal]
Buyer   Seller (Owner)

I hereby acknowledge receipt of the earnest money herein set forth in accordance with the terms hereof and I further acknowledge that I have witnessed the due execution hereof.

....
Date   Agent

CAUTION—THE PROVISIONS CONTAINED HEREIN ARE OF SUBSTANTIAL LEGAL EFFECT, AND ALL PARTIES ARE ADVISED TO CONSULT THEIR ATTORNEYS PRIOR TO SIGNING.

N.C. Bar Assoc. Form No. 2 © 1976

STANDARD PROVISIONS

1. EARNEST MONEY: In the event this offer is not accepted, or in the event that any of the conditions hereto are not satisfied, or in the event of a breach of this contract by Seller, then the earnest money shall be returned to Buyer. In the event this offer is accepted and Buyer breaches this contract, then the earnest money shall be forfeited and paid to Seller, but such payment shall not affect any other remedies available to Seller for such breach.

2. LOAN ASSUMED: In the event a loan is assumed as part of the payment of the purchase price, then all payments due from Seller thereon must be current at closing and the principal balance assumed shall be computed as of the date of closing. The amounts shown for the assumption balance and cash at closing shall be adjusted as appropriate at closing to reflect the final computations. Buyer shall be responsible for all transfer fees and any other charges required by the lender for the assumption of the loan. The escrow account, if any, shall be purchased by Buyer.

3. PROMISSORY NOTE AND DEED OF TRUST: In the event a promissory note secured by a deed of trust is given by Buyer to Seller as part of the payment of the purchase price, the promissory note and deed of trust shall be in the form of and contain the provisions of the promissory note and deed of trust forms approved by the N. C. Bar Association as Forms 4 and 5.

4. PRORATIONS AND ADJUSTMENTS: Unless otherwise provided the following items shall be prorated and adjusted between the parties or paid at closing:

(a) Ad valorem taxes on real property shall be prorated on a calendar year basis to the date of closing.

(b) Ad valorem taxes on personal property for the entire year shall be paid by Seller.

(c) All late listing penalties, if any, shall be paid by Seller.

(d) Rents, if any, for the property shall be prorated to the date of closing.

(e) Buyer shall have the right to purchase Seller's fire insurance policy upon payment to Seller of the unearned premium therefor, if the policy is assignable.

(f) Accrued, but unpaid, interest and other charges to Seller, if any, shall be computed to the date of closing and paid by Seller; interest and other charges prepaid by Seller shall be credited to Seller at closing and paid by Buyer.

5. FIRE OR OTHER CASUALTY: The risk of loss or damage by fire or other casualty prior to closing shall be upon Seller.

6. CONDITIONS:
(a) The property must be in substantially the same condition at closing as on the date of this offer, reasonable wear and tear excepted.

(b) All deeds of trust, liens and other charges against the real or personal property, not assumed by Buyer, must be paid and cancelled by Seller prior to or at closing.

(c) Title must be delivered at closing by warranty deed and must be fee simple marketable title, free of all encumbrances except ad valorem taxes for the current year (prorated to date of closing), utility easements and unviolated restrictive covenants that do not materially affect the value of the property and such other encumbrances as may be assumed or specifically approved by Buyer. The subject property must have legal access to a public right of way.

(d) If a portion of the purchase price for the property is being paid by assumption of an existing loan, then the approval of the Lender for such assumption after diligent application therefor by Buyer is a condition of this contract.

7. NEW LOAN: Buyer shall be responsible for all charges made to Buyer with respect to any new loan obtained by Buyer and Seller shall have no obligation to pay any discount fee or

other charge in connection therewith unless specifically set forth in this contract.

8. UTILITIES: Unless otherwise stated herein, the electrical, plumbing, heating and cooling systems, if any, shall be in good working order at closing. Buyer has the option to have the same inspected at Buyer's expense and any repairs must be completed or provided for by Seller at Seller's expense. Closing shall constitute acceptance of the same in their existing condition unless provision is otherwise made in writing pursuant to this paragraph.

9. TERMITES, ETC: Unless otherwise stated herein, Seller shall provide at Seller's expense a statement showing the absence of termites, wood destroying insects and organisms and structural damage therefrom on Standard Form No. 1 in accordance with the regulations of the North Carolina Structural Pest Control Committee, or if new construction, a new construction termite bond. All extermination required and repair of damage therefrom shall be paid for by Seller and completed prior to closing, unless otherwise agreed in writing by the parties.

10. LABOR OR MATERIAL: Seller shall furnish at closing an affidavit and indemnification agreement in form satisfactory to Buyer showing that all labor or materials, if any, furnished to the property within 120 days prior to the date of closing have been paid and agreeing to indemnify Buyer against all loss from any cause arising therefrom.

11. FUEL OIL: Buyer agrees to purchase from Seller the fuel oil, if any, situated in a tank on the premises for the prevailing rate per gallon with the cost of measurement thereof, if any, being borne by Seller.

12. CLOSING EXPENSES: Seller shall pay for the preparation of a deed and for the revenue stamps required by law. Buyer shall pay for recording the deed and for preparation and recording of all instruments required to secure the balance of the purchase price unpaid at closing.

13. EVIDENCE OF TITLE: Seller agrees to deliver to Buyer as soon as reasonably possible after the acceptance of this offer copies of all title information in possession of or available to Seller, including but not limited to: title insurance policies, attorney's opinions on title, surveys, covenants, deeds, notes and deeds of trust and easements relating to the real and personal property described above.

14. ASSIGNMENT: This contract may not be assigned without the written agreement of all parties, but if the same is assigned by agreement, then the same shall be binding on the Assignee and his heirs.

15. PARTIES: This contract shall be binding upon and shall inure to the benefit of the parties and their heirs. The provisions herein contained with respect to promissory notes and deeds of trust shall be binding upon and shall inure to the benefit of all parties to the same as well as subsequent owners of the property and the said notes and deeds of trust. As used herein, words in the singular include the plural and the masculine includes the feminine and neuter genders, as appropriate.

16. SURVIVAL: Any provision herein contained which by its nature and effect if required to be observed, kept, or performed after the closing shall survive the closing and remain binding upon and for the benefit of the parties hereto until fully observed, kept, or performed.

17. ENTIRE AGREEMENT: Buyer acknowledges that he has inspected the above described property. This contract contains the entire agreement of the parties and there are no representations, inducements or other provisions other than those expressed in writing. All changes, additions or deletions hereto must be in writing and signed by all parties. Nothing herein contained shall alter any agreement between a realtor and the Seller as contained in any listing contract or other agreement between them. Any party may cause this contract to be recorded.

SEAL-STAMP

Use Black Ink

NORTH CAROLINA, COUNTY OF _____

I, _____, a Notary Public of the County and State aforesaid, certify that _____ personally came before me this day and, being duly sworn, stated that in his presence _____

_____

duly executed the foregoing instrument/acknowledged the due execution of the foregoing instrument.

Witness my hand and official stamp or seal, this _____ day of _____, 19_____.

My Commission expires: _____   _____ Notary Public

SEAL-STAMP

Use Black Ink

NORTH CAROLINA, COUNTY OF _____

I, _____, a Notary Public of the County and State aforesaid, certify that _____, personally came before me this day and acknowledged that __ __ he is _____ Secretary of _____ a North Carolina corporation, and that by authority duly given and as the act of the corporation, the foregoing instrument was signed in its name by its _____ President, sealed with its corporate seal and attested by_____ as its _____Secretary.

Witness my hand and official stamp or seal, this_____day of_____, 19_____.

My commission expires: _____   _____ Notary Public

N.C. Bar Assoc. Form No. 2 © 1976

title to Byers, and the law does recognize, therefore, that Byers has something more than just the hope of obtaining title. We say that Byers has "equitable title;" this is not "legal title," which he will get at the date of closing, but a special status the purchaser has between the time a contract of sale is entered into, and the time when legal title is actually transferred.

This special status gives the purchaser the "insurable interest" that is required for one to insure property. This may be of great importance in a situation where something happens to the property before the title closing date. In many states, the purchaser bears the risk of loss in case the property is destroyed between the time the contract of sale is executed and the date title is closed. If the contract does not provide that the seller assumes this risk of loss, the purchaser had best protect himself by obtaining insurance on the property.

North Carolina, as well as a number of other states, has adopted The Uniform Vendor and Purchaser Risk Act. This statute provides that if the purchaser has not yet taken title or possession, and the property is destroyed, the contract cannot be enforced by the seller and the purchaser is entitled to the return of any deposit.

Note that the purchaser, in order to be protected by this statute, must not have taken possession. If possession is given to him, even though title has not yet passed, he will be legally obligated to go through with the deal, even if the property is destroyed. In such a situation, you can readily see the importance of insurance coverage.

We can say, therefore, that the typical contract of sale calls for the transfer of title at a date perhaps a few weeks after the contract is executed.

There is another type of contract we should be aware of. It most typically involves the purchase of unimproved property (vacant land) and calls for payment in installments, with delivery of the deed (actual transfer of title) when the final installment has been paid. This type of arrangement is called a *land contract,* sometimes also called a *contract for deed.*

Usually the buyer is given the right to possession so long as he continues to make his installment payments. There is usually a provision for the seller's protection, providing that if the buyer defaults in his payments, all of his prior installment payments are deemed to be rent, and are therefore not returnable to him.

For the buyer's protection, it is wise to arrange for the deed to be held in *escrow,* during the period of the installment payments. (Escrow describes a situation in which something is held by a third party, pending the performance or completion of some contractual obligation). The buyer is thereby protected in case of the seller's death or insolvency, and is spared the trouble and expense of establishing his claims though litigation.

4.

FINANCING REAL PROPERTY

The word "mortgage" has had, for many persons, a sinister sound, not only because of the financial implications, but because they never have fully comprehended what the term means. This is because the mortgage arrangement, while simple in itself, is often a part of other involvements so complex that the result may be one of total confusion.

Let us strip the matter down to its basic essentials.

Regardless of the purpose for which you need the money, if you approach your bank or other lending institution for a loan, they will undoubtedly want you to put up some "security" for the loan, something that the lender could sell, in the event you fail to repay the loan, and thus get his money back.

In real estate situations, the mortgage is the means by which you put up real property as security for a loan. It does not matter whether you need the loan to buy property, or to add some improvement to property you already own, or for a purpose totally unrelated to real estate.

Most buyers of real property do not have in cash the total purchase price. In fact, even in the relatively rare situations where they do, it is often desirable not to use all cash, but to borrow a substantial portion of the purchase price.

When this money is borrowed, the lender will require that the buyer execute a promissory note, which is a written expression of a promise to pay a certain amount at some future specified time, at a certain rate of interest. (In some states, a "bond" is executed, rather than a note; the result is the same.) The *note* represents the debt, or obligation to pay. (A typical note is shown on the following page.)

Now, what is the security for this debt? The borrower puts up as security the real property. Perhaps he is using the borrowed money to buy the very property to be used as security for his debt. This is the situation we are most familiar with.

PROMISSORY NOTE

.... N. C.

$_____   ...., 19.........

FOR VALUE RECEIVED the undersigned, jointly and severally, promise to pay to ....

....

.... or order,

the principal sum of

DOLLARS ($), with interest from   , at the rate of

per cent per annum on the unpaid balance until paid or until default, both principal and interest payable in lawful money of the United States, at

the office of ....

....

or at such other place as the legal holder hereof may designate in writing. It is understood and agreed that additional amounts may be advanced by the holder hereof as provided in the instruments, if any, securing this note and such advances will be added to the principal of this note and will accrue interest at the above specified rate of interest from the date of advance until paid. The principal and interest shall be due and payable as follows:

In the event of default in payment of any installment of principal or interest hereof or default under the terms of any instrument securing this note, and if the default is not made good within fifteen (15) days, the holder may, without notice, declare the remainder of the debt at once due and payable. Failure to exercise this option shall not constitute a waiver of the right to exercise the same at any other time. The principal of this note and any part thereof, and accrued interest, if any, shall bear interest at the rate of............per cent per annum after default until paid.

All parties to this note, whether principal, surety, guarantor or endorsers, hereby waive presentment for payment, demand, protest and notice of dishonor, and all defenses on the ground of extension of time for the payment hereof, which may be given by the holder of the note to them or either of them, or to anyone who has assumed the payment of this note.

Upon default the holder of this note may employ an attorney to enforce the holder's rights and remedies and the maker, principal, surety, guarantor and endorsers of this note hereby agree to pay to the holder the sum of fifteen (15%) per cent of the outstanding balance owing on said note for reasonable attorneys' fees, plus all other reasonable expenses incurred by the holder in exercising any of the holder's rights and remedies upon default.

This note is to be governed and construed in accordance with the laws of the State of North Carolina.

This note is given ...., and is secured by a

....

which is a .... lien upon the property therein described. The provisions of all security instruments securing this note are incorporated herein by reference.

IN TESTIMONY WHEREOF, each corporate maker has caused this

instrument to be executed in its corporate name by its...................

.............President, attested by its...............................
Secretary, and its corporate seal to be hereto affixed, all by order of its Board of Directors first duly given, this day and year first above written.

....
                         (Corporate Name)

By: ....

............................President

ATTEST:

....

............................Secretary (Corporate Seal)

....
                         (Corporate Name)

By: ....

............................President

ATTEST:

....

............................Secretary (Corporate Seal)

IN TESTIMONY WHEREOF, each individual maker has hereunto set his hand and adopted as his seal the word "SEAL" appearing beside his name, this day and year first above written.

....(SEAL)

....(SEAL)

....(SEAL)

....(SEAL)

....(SEAL)

....(SEAL)

....(SEAL)

N.C. Bar Assoc. Form No. 4 © 1976

The borrower executes a document by which the lender will have the right, in the event the borrower does not repay the loan as called for, to have the property sold, and the proceeds used to repay the loan.

This security arrangement is referred to as mortgaging the property.

Here is an appropriate point at which to correct a common misconception. The mortgage is *not* the debt. The promissory note (or bond) *is*. The mortgage is simply the security arrangement for the debt. Suppose the borrower defaults on his repayment; the lender could, if he so desired, simply sue the borrower personally on the note, ignoring the mortgage completely. Of course, this is not likely, since the borrower is probably not financially capable, or he would not have defaulted on his debt in the first place. So the lender resorts to the mortgage arrangement, proceeds to have the property sold, and thus has his loan repaid. This points out the interesting legal distinction between the *personal liability* of the borrower (on the note) and the liability of the property (on the mortgage).

There are two different theories of mortgage practice in use today. Although the end result is the same, we should understand the difference, since some states follow one theory and some the other.

One is the *lien* theory, the other the *title* theory.

A lien is a right given to a creditor by statute, allowing him to resort to property of the debtor in order to satisfy the debt. Under the lien theory of mortgages, the borrower (mortgagor) retains title to the property, but merely gives the lender (mortgagee) a lien on the property—the right to have the property sold to pay the debt, in the event the borrower defaults on his obligation.

Under the title theory, the borrower actually transfers title to the property, but the title transfer will be defeated, and title returned to the borrower, when the loan is repaid.

At this point you will note we have introduced the words *mortgagor* and *mortgagee*. You should know that the borrower is the mortgagor and the lender the mortgagee, and since these are the words generally used, you will, by using them, learn to distinguish the terms without confusion.

In the lien theory states, the mortgage document is a two-party instrument, involving the borrower (mortgagor) and the lender (mortgagee). A typical mortgage is shown on the following page.

In the title theory states, including North Carolina and others, the instrument used is called a *Deed of Trust,* and is a document involving three parties, the mortgagor, trustee, and mortgagee. The mortgagor transfers title to the property to a trustee; this trustee is one who has no personal involvement in the property, but holds this title for the benefit of the mortgagee. If the loan is repaid, the deed of trust is released (can-

Standard N. Y. B. T. U. Form 8015 • 5-73-75M – Mortgage (Subordinate) Individual or Corporation.

CONSULT YOUR LAWYER BEFORE SIGNING THIS INSTRUMENT—THIS INSTRUMENT SHOULD BE USED BY LAWYERS ONLY.

THIS MORTGAGE, made the   day of   , nineteen hundred and

BETWEEN

, the mortgagor,

and

, the mortgagee,

WITNESSETH, that to secure the payment of an indebtedness in the sum of

dollars,

lawful money of the United States, to be paid

with interest thereon to be computed from the date hereof, at the rate of   per centum
per annum, and to be paid on the   day of   19   , next ensuing and
      thereafter,

according to a certain bond,
note or obligation bearing even date herewith, the mortgagor hereby mortgages to the mortgagee

ALL that certain plot, piece or parcel of land, with the buildings and improvements thereon erected, situate,
lying and being in the

TOGETHER with all right, title and interest of the mortgagor in and to the land lying in the streets and roads in front of and adjoining said premises;

TOGETHER with all fixtures, chattels and articles of personal property now or hereafter attached to or used in connection with said premises, including but not limited to furnaces, boilers, oil burners, radiators and piping, coal stokers, plumbing and bathroom fixtures, refrigeration, air conditioning and sprinkler systems, wash-tubs, sinks, gas and electric fixtures, stoves, ranges, awnings, screens, window shades, elevators, motors, dynamos, refrigerators, kitchen cabinets, incinerators, plants and shrubbery and all other equipment and machinery, appliances, fittings, and fixtures of every kind in or used in the operation of the buildings standing on said premises, together with any and all replacements thereof and additions thereto;

TOGETHER with all awards heretofore and hereafter made to the mortgagor for taking by eminent domain the whole or any part of said premises or any easement therein, including any awards for changes of grade of streets, which said awards are hereby assigned to the mortgagee, who is hereby authorized to collect and receive the proceeds of such awards and to give proper receipts and acquittances therefor, and to apply the same toward the payment of the mortgage debt, notwithstanding the fact that the amount owing thereon may not then be due and payable; and the said mortgagor hereby agrees, upon request, to make, execute and deliver any and all assignments and other instruments sufficient for the purpose of assigning said awards to the mortgagee, free, clear and discharged of any encumbrances of any kind or nature whatsoever.

AND the mortgagor covenants with the mortgagee as follows:

1.   That the mortgagor will pay the indebtedness as hereinbefore provided.

2.   That the mortgagor will keep the buildings on the premises insured against loss by fire for the benefit of the mortgagee; that he will assign and deliver the policies to the mortgagee; and that he will reimburse the mortgagee for any premiums paid for insurance made by the mortgagee on the mortgagor's default in so insuring the buildings or in so assigning and delivering the policies.

3.   That no building on the premises shall be altered, removed or demolished without the consent of the mortgagee.

4.   That the whole of said principal sum and interest shall become due at the option of the mortgagee: after default in the payment of any instalment of principal or of interest for fifteen days; or after default in the payment of any tax, water rate, sewer rent or assessment for thirty days after notice and demand; or after default after notice and demand either in assigning and delivering the policies insuring the buildings against loss by fire or in reimbursing the mortgagee for premiums paid on such insurance, as hereinbefore provided; or after default upon request in furnishing a statement of the amount due on the mortgage and whether any offsets or defenses exist against the mortgage debt, as hereinafter provided. An assessment which has been made payable in instalments at the application of the mortgagor or lessee of the premises shall nevertheless, for the purpose of this paragraph, be deemed due and payable in its entirety on the day the first instalment becomes due or payable or a lien.

5.   That the holder of this mortgage, in any action to foreclose it, shall be entitled to the appointment of a receiver.

6.   That the mortgagor will pay all taxes, assessments, sewer rents or water rates, and in default thereof, the mortgagee may pay the same.

7.   That the mortgagor within five days upon request in person or within ten days upon request by mail will furnish a written statement duly acknowledged of the amount due on this mortgage and whether any offsets or defenses exist against the mortgage debt.

8.   That notice and demand or request may be in writing and may be served in person or by mail.

9.   That the mortgagor warrants the title to the premises.

10.   That the fire insurance policies required by paragraph No. 2 above shall contain the usual extended coverage endorsement; that in addition thereto the mortgagor, within thirty days after notice and demand, will keep the premises insured against war risk and any other hazard that may reasonably be required by the mortgagee All of the provisions of paragraphs No. 2 and No. 4 above relating to fire insurance and the provisions of Section 254 of the Real Property Law construing the same shall apply to the additional insurance required by this paragraph.

11.   That in case of a foreclosure sale, said premises, or so much thereof as may be affected by this mortgage, may be sold in one parcel.

12.   That if any action or proceeding be commenced (except an action to foreclose this mortgage or to collect the debt secured thereby), to which action or proceeding the mortgagee is made a party, or in which it becomes necessary to defend or uphold the lien of this mortgage, all sums paid by the mortgagee for the expense of any litigation to prosecute or defend the rights and lien created by this mortgage (including reasonable counsel fees), shall be paid by the mortgagor, together with interest thereon at the rate of six per cent. per annum and any such sum and the interest thereon shall be a lien on said premises, prior to any right, or title to, interest in or claim upon said premises attaching or accruing subsequent to the lien of this mortgage, and shall be deemed to be secured by this mortgage. In any action or proceeding to foreclose this mortgage, or to recover or collect the debt secured thereby, the provisions of law respecting the recovering of costs, disbursements and allowances shall prevail unaffected by this covenant.

13. That the mortgagor hereby assigns to the mortgagee the rents, issues and profits of the premises as further security for the payment of said indebtedness, and the mortgagor grants to the mortgagee the right to enter upon and to take possession of the premises for the purpose of collecting the same and to let the premises or any part thereof, and to apply the rents, issues and profits, after payment of all necessary charges and expenses, on account of said indebtedness. This assignment and grant shall continue in effect until this mortgage is paid. The mortgagee hereby waives the right to enter upon and to take possession of said premises for the purpose of collecting said rents, issues and profits, and the mortgagor shall be entitled to collect and receive said rents, issues and profits until default under any of the covenants, conditions or agreements contained in this mortgage, and agrees to use such rents, issues and profits in payment of principal and interest becoming due on this mortgage and in payment of taxes, assessments, sewer rents, water rates and carrying charges becoming due against said premises, but such right of the mortgagor may be revoked by the mortgagee upon any default, on five days' written notice. The mortgagor will not, without the written consent of the mortgagee, receive or collect rent from any tenant of said premises or any part thereof for a period of more than one month in advance, and in the event of any default under this mortgage will pay monthly in advance to the mortgagee, or to any receiver appointed to collect said rents, issues and profits, the fair and reasonable rental value for the use and occupation of said premises or of such part thereof as may be in the possession of the mortgagor, and upon default in any such payment will vacate and surrender the possession of said premises to the mortgagee or to such receiver, and in default thereof may be evicted by summary proceedings.

14. That the whole of said principal sum and the interest shall become due at the option of the mortgagee: (a) after failure to exhibit to the mortgagee, within ten days after demand, receipts showing payment of all taxes, water rates, sewer rents and assessments; or (b) after the actual or threatened alteration, demolition or removal of any building on the premises without the written consent of the mortgagee; or (c) after the assignment of the rents of the premises or any part thereof without the written consent of the mortgagee; or (d) if the buildings on said premises are not maintained in reasonably good repair; or (e) after failure to comply with any requirement or order or notice of violation of law or ordinance issued by any governmental department claiming jurisdiction over the premises within three months from the issuance thereof; or (f) if on application of the mortgagee two or more fire insurance companies lawfully doing business in the State of New York refuse to issue policies insuring the buildings on the premises; or (g) in the event of the removal, demolition or destruction in whole or in part of any of the fixtures, chattels or articles of personal property covered hereby, unless the same are promptly replaced by similar fixtures, chattels and articles of personal property at least equal in quality and condition to those replaced, free from chattel mortgages or other encumbrances thereon and free from any reservation of title thereto; or (h) after thirty days' notice to the mortgagor, in the event of the passage of any law deducting from the value of land for the purposes of taxation any lien thereon, or changing in any way the taxation of mortgages or debts secured thereby for state or local purposes; or (i) if the mortgagor fails to keep, observe and perform any of the other covenants, conditions or agreements contained in this mortgage; or (j) if the mortgagor fails to keep, observe and perform any of the covenants, conditions or agreements contained in any prior mortgage or fails to repay to the mortgagee the amount of any instalment of principal or interest which the mortgagee may have paid on such mortgage with interest thereon as provided in paragraph 16 of this mortgage.

15. That the mortgagor will, in compliance with Section 13 of the Lien Law, receive the advances secured hereby and will hold the right to receive such advances as a trust fund to be applied first for the purpose of paying the cost of the improvement and will apply the same first to the payment of the cost of the improvement before using any part of the total of the same for any other purpose.

16. If the mortgagor fails to pay any instalment of principal or interest on any prior mortgage when the same becomes due, the mortgagee may pay the same, and the mortgagor on demand will repay the amount so paid with interest thereon at the legal rate and the same shall be added to the mortgage indebtedness and be secured by this mortgage.

Strike out clause 17 if inapplicable.

17. That the execution of this mortgage has been duly authorized by the board of directors of the mortgagor.

18. This mortgage is subject and subordinate to

This mortgage may not be changed or terminated orally. The covenants contained in this mortgage shall run with the land and bind the mortgagor, the heirs, personal representatives, successors and assigns of the mortgagor and all subsequent owners, encumbrancers, tenants and subtenants of the premises, and shall enure to the benefit of the mortgagee, the personal representatives, successors and assigns of the mortgagee and all subsequent holders of this mortgage. The word "mortgagor" shall be construed as if it read "mortgagors" and the word "mortgagee" shall be construed as if it read "mortgagees" whenever the sense of this mortgage so requires.

IN WITNESS WHEREOF, this mortgage has been duly executed by the mortgagor

IN PRESENCE OF:

STATE OF NEW YORK, COUNTY OF   **ss:**

On the   day of   19   , before me
personally came

to me known to be the individual   described in and who
executed the foregoing instrument, and acknowledged that
executed the same.

STATE OF NEW YORK, COUNTY OF   **ss:**

On the   day of   19   , before me
personally came

to me known to be the individual   described in and who
executed the foregoing instrument, and acknowledged that
executed the same.

STATE OF NEW YORK, COUNTY OF   **ss:**

On the   day of   19   , before me
personally came
to me known, who, being by me duly sworn, did depose and
say that   he resides at No.
                                                    ;
that   he is the
of
                                   , the corporation described
in and which executed the foregoing instrument; that   he
knows the seal of said corporation; that the seal affixed
to said instrument is such corporate seal; that it was so
affixed by order of the board of directors of said corporation, and that   he signed h   name thereto by like order.

STATE OF NEW YORK, COUNTY OF   **ss:**

On the   day of   19   , before me
personally came
the subscribing witness to the foregoing instrument, with
whom I am personally acquainted, who, being by me duly
sworn, did depose and say that   he resides at No.
                                                    ;
that   he knows

                                          to be the individual
described in and who executed the foregoing instrument;
that   he, said subscribing witness, was present and saw
              execute the same; and that   he, said witness,
at the same time subscribed h   name as witness thereto

Mortgage
(SUBORDINATE)

TITLE NO.

TO

SECTION
BLOCK
LOT
COUNTY OR TOWN

Recorded At Request of The Title Guarantee Company
RETURN BY MAIL TO:

Zip No.

RESERVE THIS SPACE FOR USE OF RECORDING OFFICE

celled), and is no longer in effect. If, on the other hand, the mortgagor defaults in repaying the loan, there is usually a "power of sale" clause in the deed of trust which gives the trustee the right to proceed to have the property sold. He must comply with statutory requirements as to the proper procedure, but this power of sale clause avoids the necessity for the trustee to start a court proceeding to establish the right to have the property sold.

A typical Deed of Trust is shown on the following page.

The procedure by which the mortgagor's property is reached is called *foreclosure*. This is done, of course, for the benefit of the mortgagee. The sale of the property is therefore a foreclosure sale.

The word "foreclosure" refers to the fact that the right of the mortgagor to regain his property is being foreclosed, or cut off. Until that point, the mortgagor has the right, by paying whatever is past due, plus interest and expenses, to "redeem" his property. This right is known as the *equity of redemption,* and the time period during which he may exercise this right varies among the states. In some states he even has a period of time *after* the foreclosure sale within which to redeem the property. In North Carolina, as in most states, his right of redemption ends with the foreclosure sale.

Let us suppose that Mr. Baker borrows $20,000 from the Bank of Jonesville, and mortgages his property to the bank. Let us further suppose that Baker defaults in his obligation to repay, and there is a subsequent foreclosure sale, at which the property is sold for $18,000. The bank may now sue Baker and obtain a deficiency judgment against him for $2,000. Since a judgment becomes a lien against any assets of the judgment debtor, the bank would now have additional means of obtaining payment of Baker's debt in full.

Types of Mortgages

Term Mortgage. A mortgage for a specified term, usually not longer than five years, which carries no provision for repayment of the principal until the end of the term. Interest is paid at specified intervals—perhaps monthly, or quarterly, or semiannually—and then, at the end of the term, the borrower must repay the entire amount of the loan unless the lender agrees to renewal of the mortgage. This was the common type of mortgage used until the Depression of the 1930's, when many mortgagors were unable to make the repayment of principal when their mortgage loans came due.

SATISFACTION: The debt secured by the within Deed of Trust together with the note(s) secured thereby has been satisfied in full.

This the .... day of ...., 19.........

Signed: ....

Recording: Time, Book and Page

Tax Lot No. .... Parcel Identifier No. ....

Verified by .... County on the .... day of ...., 19........

by ....

Mail after recording to ....

....

This instrument was prepared by ....

NORTH CAROLINA DEED OF TRUST

THIS DEED of TRUST made this   day of   , 19   , by and between:

GRANTOR	TRUSTEE	BENEFICIARY

Enter in appropriate block for each party: name, address, and, if appropriate, character of entity, e.g. corporation or partnership.

The designation Grantor, Trustee, and Beneficiary as used herein shall include said parties, their heirs, successors, and assigns, and shall include singular, plural, masculine, feminine or neuter as required by context.

WITNESSETH, That whereas the Grantor is indebted to the Beneficiary in the principal sum of ....

.... Dollars ($................),
as evidenced by a promissory note of even date herewith, the terms of which are incorporated herein by reference. The final due date for payment

of said promissory note, if not sooner paid, is ....

NOW, THEREFORE, as security for said debt and a valuable consideration, receipt of which is hereby acknowledged, the Grantor has bargained, sold, given, granted and conveyed and does by these presents bargain, sell, give, grant and convey to said Trustee, his heirs, or successors, and assigns,

the parcel(s) of land situated in .... Township,

County of ...., State of North Carolina, and more particularly described as follows:

N.C. Bar Assoc. Form No. 5 © 1976

TO HAVE AND TO HOLD said real property with all privileges and appurtenances thereunto belonging, to the said Trustee, his heirs, successors, and assigns forever, upon the trusts, terms and conditions, and for the uses hereinafter set forth.

If the Grantor shall pay the note secured hereby in accordance with its terms, together with interest thereon, and any renewals or extensions thereof in whole or in part, and shall comply with all of the covenants, terms, and conditions of this deed of trust, then this conveyance shall be null and void and may be cancelled of record at the request of the Grantor. If, however, there shall be any default in any of the covenants, terms, or conditions of the note secured hereby, or any failure or neglect to comply with the covenants, terms, or conditions contained in this deed of trust, then and in any of such events, if the default is not made good within fifteen (15) days, the note shall, at the option of the Beneficiary, at once become due and payable without notice, and it shall be lawful for and the duty of the Trustee, upon request of the Beneficiary, to sell the land herein conveyed at public auction for cash, after having first given such notice of hearing as to commencement of foreclosure proceedings and obtained such findings or leave of court as may be then required by law and giving such notice and advertising the time and place of such sale in such manner as may be then provided by law, and upon such and any resales and upon compliance with the then law relating to foreclosure proceedings to convey title to the purchaser in fee simple.

The proceeds of the Sale shall after the Trustee retains his commission be applied to the costs of sale, the amount due on the note hereby secured and otherwise as required by the then existing law relating to foreclosures. The Trustee's commission shall be five per cent of the gross proceeds of the sale or the minimum sum of $................., whichever is greater, for a completed foreclosure. In the event foreclosure is commenced, but not completed, the Grantor shall pay all expenses incurred by Trustee and a partial commission computed on five per cent of the outstanding indebtedness or the above stated minimum sum, whichever is greater, in accordance with the following schedule, to wit: one-fourth thereof before the Trustee issues a notice of hearing on the right to foreclose; one-half thereof after issuance of said notice; three-fourths thereof after such hearing; and the greater of the full commission or minimum after the initial sale.

And the said Grantor does hereby covenant and agree with the Trustee and with the Beneficiary as follows:

1. INSURANCE. Grantor shall keep all improvements on said land, now or hereafter erected, constantly insured for the benefit of the Beneficiary against loss by fire, windstorm and such other casualties and contingencies, in such manner and in such companies and for such amounts, not exceeding the amount due on the Note secured hereby, as may be satisfactory to the Beneficiary. Grantor shall purchase such insurance, pay all premiums therefor, and shall deliver to Beneficiary such policies along with evidence of premium payment as long as the Note secured hereby remains unpaid. If Grantor fails to purchase such insurance, pay the premiums therefor or deliver said policies along with evidence of payment of premiums thereon, then Beneficiary, at his option, may purchase such insurance. Such amounts paid by Beneficiary shall be added to the Note secured by this Deed of Trust, and shall be due and payable upon demand by Grantor to Beneficiary.

2. TAXES, ASSESSMENTS, CHARGES. Grantor shall pay all taxes, assessments and charges as may be lawfully levied against said premises within thirty (30) days after the same shall become due. In the event that Grantor fails to so pay all taxes, assessments and charges as herein required, then Beneficiary, at his option, may pay the same and the amounts so paid shall be added to the Note, secured by this Deed of Trust, and shall be due and payable upon demand by Grantor to Beneficiary.

3. PARTIAL RELEASE. Grantor shall not be entitled to the partial release of any of the above described property unless a specific provision providing therefor is included in this Deed of Trust. In the event a partial release provision is included in this Deed of Trust, Grantor must strictly comply with the terms thereof. Notwithstanding anything herein contained, Grantor shall not be entitled to any release of property unless Grantor is not in default and is in full compliance with all of the terms and provisions of the Note, this Deed of Trust, and any other instrument that may be securing said Note.

4. WASTE. The Grantor covenants that he will keep the premises herein conveyed in as good order, repair and condition as they are now, reasonable wear and tear excepted, and that he will not commit or permit any waste.

5. WARRANTIES. Grantor covenants with Trustee and Beneficiary that he is seized of the premises in fee simple, has the right to convey the same in fee simple, that title is marketable and free and clear of all encumbrances, and that he will warrant and defend the title against the lawful claims of all persons whomsoever, except for the exceptions hereinafter stated. Title to the property hereinabove described is subject to the following exceptions:

6. SUBSTITUTION OF TRUSTEE. Grantor and Trustee covenant and agree to and with Beneficiary that in case the said Trustee, or any successor trustee, shall die, become incapable of acting, renounce his trust, or for other similar or dissimilar reason become unacceptable to the holder of the Note, then the holder of the Note may appoint, in writing, a trustee to take the place of the Trustee; and upon the probate and registration of the same, the trustee thus appointed shall succeed to all the rights, powers, and duties of the Trustee.

7. CIVIL ACTION. In the event that the Trustee is named as a party to any civil action as trustee in this Deed of Trust, the Trustee shall be entitled to employ an attorney at law, including himself if he is a licensed attorney, to represent him in said action and the reasonable attorney's fees of the Trustee in such action shall be paid by Beneficiary and charged to the Note and secured by this Deed of Trust.

8. PRIOR LIENS: Default under the terms of any instrument secured by a lien to which this deed of trust is subordinate shall constitute default hereunder.

IN WITNESS WHEREOF, the Grantor has hereunto set his hand and seal, or if corporate, has caused this instrument to be signed in its corporate name by its duly authorized officers and its seal to be hereunto affixed by authority of its Board of Directors, the day and year first above written.

(Corporate Name) ....

USE BLACK INK ONLY

....(SEAL)

By: ....

....(SEAL)

...........................President

....(SEAL)

ATTEST:

....(SEAL)

...........................Secretary (Corporate Seal)

SEAL-STAMP

Use Black Ink

STATE OF NORTH CAROLINA ....COUNTY...............

I, ..., a notary public of said county do hereby certify that ....

.... Grantor, personally appeared before me this day and acknowledged the execution of the foregoing instrument. Witness my hand and official stamp or seal, this............. day of............................, 19.........

My commission expires: .... Notary Public

SEAL-STAMP

Use Black Ink

NORTH CAROLINA, COUNTY OF ....

I, ..., a Notary Public of the County and State aforesaid, certify that ...., personally came before me this day and acknowledged that .... .. he is .... Secretary of .... a North Carolina corporation, and that by authority duly given and as the act of the corporation, the foregoing instrument was signed in its name by its .... President, sealed with its corporate seal and attested by .... as its ....Secretary.

Witness my hand and official stamp or seal, this ....day of............................, 19.........

My commission expires: .... Notary Public

The foregoing Certificate(s) of ....

....

....

is/are certified to be correct. This instrument and this certificate are duly registered at the date and time and in the Book and Page shown on the first page hereof.

............................REGISTER OF DEEDS FOR............................COUNTY

By ....Deputy/Assistant - Register of Deeds

N.C. Bar Assoc. Form No. 5 © 1976

Amortized Mortgage. To "amortize" an obligation is to repay it in specified installments over a certain period of time. This is the type of mortgage commonly used today. In the typical home mortgage loan, the borrower makes a monthly payment of a constant amount over a period of years. Each installment includes not only a payment of interest, but an amount toward repayment of the principal. Each payment, therefore, allocates a gradually increasing portion of the payment to principal, and a gradually decreasing portion to interest. (This is so because, with each payment, the remaining balance of the principal amount of the loan decreases, thereby decreasing the amount of interest payable.) Based upon the rate of interest carried by the loan, the monthly payment is pre-determined, so that at the expiration date of the loan term the principal balance becomes zero.

Purchase Money Mortgage. Here the purchaser gives a mortgage to the seller as part of the purchase price of the property. (The seller is said to "take back" a mortgage.) In other words, the seller becomes the mortgagee. In some situations, this comes about when the purchaser has a limited amount of cash to put up and the amount of the mortgage loan he can obtain from a lending institution is insufficient to cover the balance of the purchase price. The seller might take back a *second* mortgage, which is nothing more than an additional obligation for which the property is being put up as security. A second mortgage is a *junior* lien against the property, which means that it is secondary to the senior or first mortgage. (In the event of a foreclosure sale of the property, the first mortgagee is entitled to have his debt satisfied before any funds are available for the second mortgage.)

To illustrate this situation—let us suppose that the property is being sold for $40,000. Buyer has $5,000 cash and is able to obtain a mortgage loan of $30,000 only. He is still $5,000 short, but perhaps the seller will take back a purchase money second mortgage of $5,000 to assure the deal. Of course, a purchase money mortgage need not necessarily be a second mortgage. The transaction could have been concluded on the basis of $5,000 down and the balance of $35,000 in the form of a purchase money mortgage taken back by the seller, who would thereby become a first mortgagee.

Package Mortgage. This mortgage covers not only the real property, but personal property as well—perhaps equipment, appliances, etc.

Blanket Mortgage. This covers more than one parcel of real estate. A common example might be a blanket mortgage covering all the lots in a residential subdivision. As the developer sells each lot, he pays the mortgagee a previously agreed upon amount, and the mortgagee releases that lot from the mortgage lien he holds.

Construction Mortgage. In order to finance building construction, mortgage loans are arranged by which money is advanced by the lender in stages, as the construction progresses. The builder "draws" against the loan amount in accordance with a pre-arranged schedule of stages of completion of the structure.

Open-end Mortgage. Actually, the typical construction loan is an example of an open-end mortgage (sometimes referred to as a "mortgage for future advances"). In the open-end mortgage, the mortgagor may obtain additional funds at a later time, so long as the total obligation does not exceed the amount originally approved.

In some cases, where so agreed, the borrower, after he has repaid a portion of the loan, may "re-borrow" on terms agreed upon, up to the amount of the original loan.

Wrap-around Mortgage. This is an interesting concept involving a new mortgage loan that is made against a property with an existing mortgage already against it. But instead of the new loan simply being a second mortgage that has junior standing, the new mortgage "wraps around," or includes, the first mortgage.

To illustrate—suppose the owner has an old existing mortgage of $200,000 at 6% interest, on property whose market value is now $500,000. Interest rates are, let us say, at 9% currently, and the owner-borrower cannot, for one reason or another, refinance the existing loan. A lender offers to lend the borrower $300,000 at, say, 8% interest, and the *lender* will take over the payments on the old loan. The new loan "wraps around" the old one—the borrower will actually receive only $100,000, the difference between his existing obligation of $200,000 and the amount of the new loan, $300,000.

The borrower thereby obtains his additional funds, and the lender benefits by having his 8% loan wrap around an existing obligation on which he will be making only 6% interest payments, thus giving him a greater net return.

This arrangement obviously is of value only at a time of high interest rates. It is commonly used in sales of commercial properties where the buyer has limited cash, and the seller might be induced to sell to him by taking back a purchase money mortgage at the current high interest rate, with the buyer assuming the existing mortgage and paying this higher interest rate on *that* loan as well; this rate is thereby wrapping around the old mortgage loan.

As we mentioned, the amortizing mortgage is most commonly used today. Many of us are making monthly payments on our homes to some lending institution, and these payments include interest on our obligation and an amount toward reduction of the principal. In addition, many institutions take care of paying the annual real property taxes and insurance on the property; this is done by including an amount in the monthly payment which, when accumulated, will be sufficient to pay the tax and insurance items as they fall due.

Who are the lenders who make the mortgage loans we have been discussing? They fall into the following categories:

Savings and Loan Associations. Second only to commercial banks in terms of total assets, these institutions make about one-half of all residential mortgage loans (one to four-family residences) in the nation. They may be federally chartered or state chartered. Within certain limitations, they may make loans up to 95% of the appraised value of property.

Commercial Banks. These institutions, although largest in total size, make only about 17% of all mortgage loans nationwide. Banks may be state chartered or federally chartered. The federally chartered banks are under more severe limitations on lending practices than are the state chartered banks.

Life Insurance Companies. Insurance companies come under strict state regulation, but their large resources, primarily their reserve funds, make them substantial investors in large commercial enterprises such as shopping centers and office buildings. Rather than lend directly from their own offices, insurance companies generally lend through mortgage bankers.

Other Sources of Mortgage Funds. Pension funds, trust funds, and individual lenders are additional sources of mortgage loans. Individual lenders are prime sources of second mortgage money, generally because of the higher interest rate. (As we have noted, this higher return is expected by the lender because of the higher risk involved.)

In times gone by, there was no such thing as "guaranteeing" or "insuring" the repayment of a mortgage loan—not unless the borrower simply had someone who would be willing to obligate himself as a co-signer of the note. We now have, however, both governmental and private assistance in this direction.

FHA Mortgage. An arrangement by which the Federal Housing Authority insures a lender against loss on mortgage loans. The FHA does *not* make the loan. This is made by a lending institution, and the property must be appraised and approved by the FHA. There is a maximum interest rate set, as well as a maximum dollar amount for which the loan may be made. In addition, there are certain rather minimal down payment requirements. The borrower must pay an annual premium for the insurance, amounting to ½ of 1% of the outstanding balance of the mortgage loan.

VA Mortgage. Veterans who are buying homes may obtain loans that are partially guaranteed by the Veterans Administration. This is not insurance requiring a premium payment; the VA simply undertakes to guarantee 60% of the loan, up to a maximum of $25,000. The loans are for 30 years, and require no down payment. Interest is usually set at a rate similar to that of the FHA mortgage.

You may question why a lender would be willing to make this loan, knowing that only 60% is guaranteed. Remember—the need for resorting to this guarantee would arise only where a lender has suffered an actual loss because the borrower defaulted, the property was sold at foreclosure, and the sale did not bring enough to satisfy the debt. Let us suppose a veteran has an outstanding mortgage loan of $30,000. Since the maximum VA guarantee is $18,000, for the lender to suffer any ultimate out-of-pocket loss, the property would have to bring at the foreclosure sale an amount under $12,000—hardly likely, when you consider that the VA, before approving the original loan, had to appraise and approve the property.

What usually happens upon a default and foreclosure sale is that the VA pays off the outstanding loan balance, takes over the property, and then sells it.

Under Congressional authority, the VA has been allowed to make direct loans to veterans in certain rural areas where financing has not been otherwise available, but such activity has not been extensive.

In rural communities not within range of urban areas, persons of moderate income who cannot obtain mortgage loans otherwise can obtain up to 100% financing from the Farmers Home Administration for the purchase of homes within certain price and structural limitations. The interest rate is generally somewhat less than the prevailing rate on conventional loans, and the repayment period is 33 years.

Conventional Mortgage. This term is used to describe a mortgage loan that is not guaranteed or insured by some agency of government. The interest rate will be higher than the FHA or VA mortgage, and the borrower will usually need a higher down payment. We saw that VA loans could be 100% loans (100% of the appraised value, thus requiring no down payments). In conventional mortgages this "loan-to-value ratio" (the amount of the loan expressed as a percentage of appraised valuation) generally has a maximum of 80%. In other words, on a $40,000 property, the maximum conventional loan would be $32,000. However, with the advent of private mortgage insurance companies, it became possible for lenders to make 90% and even 95% loans. Buyers can thereby obtain their homes with 5% or 10% down payments.

Under private mortgage insurance, the borrower pays an insurance premium for insuring the top 20% or 25% of the loan. The insurance continues until the loan is reduced to the point where the balance is only 75% of the property value.

Repayment of Loans. We have been considering loan repayment periods of 20, 25, 30 years and more, but it is possible that a borrower may wish to repay the entire debt before the end of the period originally agreed on. This right of *prepayment* does not exist unless given to the borrower in the original mortgage agreement, and even then the lender may impose conditions or restrictions.

For example, it is common for a lender to require a penalty of some amount if the borrower prepays the entire loan balance, perhaps 2% of the outstanding loan balance. Thus, a borrower whose original loan was $30,000 which has now been reduced to $26,000 would, under those conditions, have to pay $520 along with his $26,000 prepayment.

Some states limit the lender's right to impose prepayment penalties. In North Carolina, if the original loan was $100,000 or less, the lender cannot charge a prepayment penalty after three years. Even during the first three years of the loan, the maximum penalty allowed is 2% of the outstanding balance.

Federally chartered Savings and Loan Associations are prohibited from charging prepayment penalties, nor are there prepayment charges under FHA or VA loans.

In connection with this topic, we should take note of the terms *open* or *closed* mortgage. An *open* mortgage is one which by its terms can be paid off before maturity. A *closed* mortgage is one which cannot.

In periods of inflation, with a corresponding rise in interest rates, many institutions are earning relatively low yields on their long-term mortgage loans made earlier, while paying relatively high interest rates to their depositors. In addition, since borrowers are repaying their loans with inflation-affected ''cheaper'' dollars (in terms of purchasing power), these institutions have devised plans by which the rate of interest on a mortgage is tied to some agreed-upon, publicly announced index of measurement. These mortgages are called *variable rate* mortgages, and the rate of interest could periodically move up or down (within certain guaranteed limits) as the index warranted. This type of mortgage has received only very limited approval in a few states.

Points. Few topics are as confusing to most as the subject of *points.* Let us try to simplify it. What we mean by the term is a charge or fee which the lender of mortgage money collects, the purpose of which is to increase the yield to him on his loan. Your next question might well be: ''If the lender wants to increase the yield on his money, why does he not simply charge a higher rate of interest?'' The answer is that he might not be allowed to do that.

To illustrate—the matter of points arises commonly in FHA or VA loans, where the interest rate is usually lower than the going rate, and obviously a lender would be unwilling to lend money at, say, 8% if he could get 9% at the going rate on conventional loans. He will want a payment of a sum which, as a result of some involved calculation, will result in his being in the same position as though he had lent the money at 9% interest.

Under FHA and VA regulations, the lender cannot charge the borrower more than 1% of the loan amount as a fee for making the loan. The *points,* therefore, must be paid by someone else (The Seller). So that if Mr. Sellars is selling his property to Mr. Beyer, who is obtaining a VA loan, Mr. Sellars had best be aware that he will probably have to pay Mr. Beyer's mortgage lender a payment of points. (In actual practice, Sellars may have taken this into account in setting his price.)

How are points calculated? A *point* is 1% of the loan amount. As a rough rule of thumb, it takes 8 points to increase a lender's yield by the equivalent of a 1% change in the interest rate. For example, if we wish to have a 6½% loan bring the lender the equivalent of a 7½% loan, we would have to charge 8 points, or 8% of the loan amount. If the loan amount were $20,000, the lender would require a payment of $1600.

In the illustration we used earlier, we described a VA or FHA maximum interest rate of 8½% as compared with a going rate of 9% on conventional loans. In such case, the lender would only charge 4 points, since he only wishes to increase the effective yield by the equivalent of an interest rate change of only ½ of 1%.

In some areas, the fee which a borrower pays a lender simply for making the loan is described in terms of *points,* but this should not be confused with what we have just described. This "mortgage origination" fee is sometimes limited by law. In North Carolina, for example, mortgage loans under $300,000 on one-family or two-family dwellings cannot carry more than a 1% charge for making the loan. State laws such as these do not, of course, affect FHA or VA situations. As mentioned earlier, those cases are controlled by the federal regulations covering those loans.

Secondary Mortgage Market. Thus far our discussion of mortgage financing has centered on the *primary* mortgage market, consisting of lenders making mortgage loans to borrowers. But there is also a *secondary* mortgage market in which institutions or individuals invest funds by buying existing mortgages from the original lenders. (Do not confuse the word "secondary" with our previous discussion of "second mortgages".)

The federal government has been active in this field primarily to promote and assure the availability of funds for mortgage loans. When existing mortgages are purchased from the original lenders, those lenders are then in a position to use those new funds to make new loans.

The Federal National Mortgage Association (FNMA, commonly referred to as "Fanny May") is a corporation privately owned, operating under federal government supervision, which buys conventional, FHA, or VA mortgages. It obtains its funds by selling securities, backed by its mortgage holdings. It also raises funds by reselling to investors mortgages it has acquired.

The Government National Mortgage Association (GNMA, or "Ginny May") is a federal agency formed primarily to purchase existing mortgages issued in connection with various low-income and other government-subsidized housing programs. In recent years, GNMA and FNMA have cooperated in a "tandem plan" by which not only subsidized programs but FHA and VA mortgages as well, are made attractive to lenders.

Primarily for Savings and Loan Associations, the Federal Home Loan Bank System (FHLB) was organized in 1932. It serves those institutions as a source of credit in much the same way that the Federal Reserve Bank serves commercial banks. All federally chartered Savings and Loan institutions are required to be members. State chartered institutions may join if they meet the qualifications. The FHLB System has formed the Federal Home Loan Mortgage Corporation ("Freddy Mac") which buys conventional mortgages (although it may also buy FHA and VA mortgages). It raises funds by selling bonds backed by its pool of mortgages.

Truth-in-Lending. The Consumer Credit Protection Act of 1968 is commonly referred to as the "Truth-in-Lending" Act. The purpose of the law is not to set loan rates, but to assure that full disclosure of all finance charges, as well as the true Annual Percentage Rate (APR) of interest, is made to borrowers.

With regard to real property mortgage loans, the law affects primarily transactions involving individuals who purchase homes, since commercial and business loans, and loans to builders and landlords, are not included.

Certain fees and charges must be included in computing the APR. While the nominal interest rate might be, for example, 8½%, let us suppose that, on a 20-year, $15,000 loan, service charges of $300 are deducted from the loan amount. While the monthly payments called for would be computed on a $15,000 loan, since the actual amount furnished is only $14,700, the true APR would be more than 8½%.

In 1974, Congress passed the Real Estate Settlement Procedures Act (RESPA), the purpose of which was to assure borrowers being provided with full knowledge of settlement procedures and costs. By 1976 its provisions had been twice amended, but in its present form it applies to all "federally regulated" mortgage lenders (thus covering virtually all lenders, since most lending institutions come under the regulation of federal agencies such as the Federal Reserve Board, Federal Deposit Insurance Corporation, Federal Home Loan Bank Board, etc.). Affected are all "federally regulated" mortgages on one-family dwellings, condominiums and cooperatives occupied by one-to-four families.

Under the requirements of the Act, the lender must furnish the borrower with a HUD information booklet which describes the procedures specified by the Act, and sets forth the practices prohibited by it. The lender must also furnish a "good faith" estimate of the closing costs the borrower may expect to be charged with. The borrower must also be given a completed HUD standardized form at the time of closing, detailing all of the financial items in connection with the loan.

A copy of this form is reproduced on the next page.

A. U.S. DEPARTMENT OF HOUSING AND URBAN DEVELOPMENT DISCLOSURE/SETTLEMENT STATEMENT	B. TYPE OF LOAN
	1. ☐ FHA 2. ☐ FMHA 3. ☐ CONV. UNINS.
	4. ☐ VA 5. ☐ CONV. INS.
	6. FILE NUMBER 7. LOAN NUMBER

If the Truth-in-Lending Act applies to this transaction, a Truth-in-Lending statement is attached as page 3 of this form.	8. MORTG. INS. CASE NO.

C. NOTE: This form is furnished to you prior to settlement to give you information about your settlement costs, and again after settlement to show the actual costs you have paid. The present copy of the form is:

☐ ADVANCE DISCLOSURE OF COSTS. Some items are estimated, and are marked "(e)". Some amounts may change if the settlement is held on a date other than the date estimated below. The preparer of this form is not responsible for errors or changes in amounts furnished by others.

☐ STATEMENT OF ACTUAL COSTS. Amounts paid to and by the settlement agent are shown. Items marked "(p.o.c.)" were paid outside the closing; they are shown here for informational purposes and are not included in totals.

D. NAME OF BORROWER	E. SELLER	F. LENDER

G. PROPERTY LOCATION	H. SETTLEMENT AGENT	I. DATES
		LOAN COMMITMENT / ADVANCE DISCLOSURE
	PLACE OF SETTLEMENT	SETTLEMENT / DATE OF PRORATIONS IF DIFFERENT FROM SETTLEMENT

J. SUMMARY OF BORROWER'S TRANSACTION		K. SUMMARY OF SELLER'S TRANSACTION	
100. GROSS AMOUNT DUE FROM BORROWER:		400. GROSS AMOUNT DUE TO SELLER:	
		401. Contract sales price	
101. Contract sales price		402. Personal property	
102. Personal property		403.	
103. Settlement charges to borrower (from line 1400, Section L)		404.	
104.		Adjustments for items paid by seller in advance:	
105.		405. City/town taxes to	
Adjustments for items paid by seller in advance:		406. County taxes to	
		407. Assessments to	
106. City/town taxes to		408. to	
107. County taxes to		409. to	
108. Assessments to		410. to	
109. to		411. to	
110. to		420. GROSS AMOUNT DUE TO SELLER	
111. to			
112. to		NOTE: The following 500 and 600 series sections are not required to be completed when this form is used for advance disclosure of settlement costs prior to settlement.	
120. GROSS AMOUNT DUE FROM BORROWER:			
200. AMOUNTS PAID BY OR IN BEHALF OF BORROWER:		500. REDUCTIONS IN AMOUNT DUE TO SELLER:	
		501. Payoff of first mortgage loan	
201. Deposit or earnest money		502. Payoff of second mortgage loan	
202. Principal amount of new loan(s)		503. Settlement charges to seller (from line 1400, Section L)	
203. Existing loan(s) taken subject to			
204.		504. Existing loan(s) taken subject to	
205.		505.	
Credits to borrower for items unpaid by seller:		506.	
		507.	
206. City/town taxes to		508.	
207. County taxes to		509.	
208. Assessments to		Credits to borrower for items unpaid by seller:	
209. to			
210. to		510. City/town taxes to	
211. to		511. County taxes to	
212. to		512. Assessments to	
220. TOTAL AMOUNTS PAID BY OR IN BEHALF OF BORROWER		513. to	
300. CASH AT SETTLEMENT REQUIRED FROM OR PAYABLE TO BORROWER:		514. to	
		515. to	
301. Gross amount due from borrower (from line 120)		520. TOTAL REDUCTIONS IN AMOUNT DUE TO SELLER:	
		600. CASH TO SELLER FROM SETTLEMENT:	
302. Less amounts paid by or in behalf of borrower (from line 220)	( )	601. Gross amount due to seller (from line 420)	
		602. Less total reductions in amount due to seller (from line 520)	( )
303. CASH (☐ REQUIRED FROM) OR (☐ PAYABLE TO) BORROWER:		603. CASH TO SELLER FROM SETTLEMENT	

HUD 1A REV 6-75 AS & AS (1323)   SPECIAL FORM OMB No. 63-R 1501

Turning to the purchase of property upon which there is an existing mortgage, we come to an interesting technicality. This involves either "assuming" the mortgage or buying "subject to" the mortgage.

Suppose Mr. Sellers is selling his home for $30,000 to Mr. Buyer and there is an existing mortgage of $24,000 on the property. Mr. Buyer could, of course, simply obtain from a lender a mortgage loan in an amount which, together with whatever cash payment he can make, will total the $30,000 price. At the title closing, Sellers would receive the $30,000 and would pay off his mortgage obligation. Buyer would thereafter make his monthly payments on the loan he had obtained.

But let us suppose that Mr. Sellers' existing mortgage was first obtained some years ago, when interest rates were, say, 6½%. If the present rate on mortgage loans is 9%, it would be advantageous for Mr. Buyer if, instead of arranging his own financing, he could take over Sellers' 6½% loan. Many loans are, by their terms, "assumable" by a buyer, and if this be so, this fact would even be a valid selling point in Mr. Sellers' attempt to sell his property.

If Mr. Sellers' mortgage permits this, Mr. Buyer could then pay Mr. Sellers $6,000 in cash and take over Sellers' $24,000 loan. Now he can do this in either of two ways. If he "assumes" the loan, he obligates himself personally to repay the debt. If there is a later default and foreclosure sale, and the sale does not bring an amount sufficient to satisfy the debt, the mortgagee may obtain a deficiency judgment against Buyer; he did, remember, promise to pay the debt.

However, Buyer could have bought the property "subject to" the mortgage. In this case, he does not assume the debt. He will continue to make the mortgage payments (he does not wish to lose the property) but in the event of a default, foreclosure sale, and a deficiency on the sale, Buyer would not be liable for a deficiency judgment. Since he did not *assume* the loan, the most that he can lose is the property.

Here is the appropriate time to correct a common misconception. Where property with an existing mortgage is transferred, whether the buyer *assumes* the mortgage or takes *subject to* the mortgage, the original mortgagor (the seller) *remains liable on the debt*. Only if the mortgagee releases him and agrees to substitute the buyer in his place, will the seller no longer have any liability. In the absence of such release, the buyer and seller are both liable, so that if the buyer defaults, the mortgagee may still look to the seller.

Again we are pointing out the difference between personal liability on the promissory note (assuming the mortgage loan) and merely continuing the liability of the property to satisfy the debt (buying subject to the mortgage).

Usually, even where mortgages may be assumed by a buyer, there is a loan assumption fee charged by the mortgagee. Unless there is a substantial difference between the loan's interest rate and the current rate, that fee will likely be a relatively small amount, perhaps $25-$50. (There may be a state law fixing a maximum fee.)

5.

LIENS AND JUDGMENTS

In the chapter on mortgages, we referred to a mortgage as an example of a lien, and we defined a lien as a right the law gives a creditor, in some instances, to satisfy his debt out of the debtor's property. Some liens existed at common law, and others have been created by statute.

Since we are concerned with real estate, we shall consider the subject of liens only as they may involve or affect real property.

We divide liens into two broad categories—*specific liens* and *general liens*.

Specific Liens. So designated, because they affect specific property. A real estate mortgage is an example of a specific lien, since a particular parcel of property has been put up as security for the loan. The lender has a lien on that piece of property, which he may exercise if the borrower defaults. The mortgage gives him no rights against any other property owned by the debtor.

Another example of a specific lien is a tax or assessment lien. If the real property tax is unpaid, the taxing authority has a lien against the specific property for which the tax was not paid. The same is true for a special assessment which is sometimes levied for an improvement such as street paving, sidewalk and curbing, etc. If the assessment is unpaid, a lien exists against the particular property against which the assessment was levied.

With regard to the tax lien, do not confuse this with the situation where a taxing body such as the federal or state Internal Revenue Service obtains a judgment for something such as unpaid income tax. That is quite another matter. What we are discussing here are *specific* liens attaching to particular parcels of property because of unpaid taxes or assessments that had been levied against those properties.

One of the most interesting and potentially troublesome specific liens is the mechanic's lien (sometimes called the laborer's and materialman's lien).

The mechanic's lien did not exist at common law; it is purely a result of statutory enactment, and the particular requirements vary from state to state, although the basic purpose is the same. It is a lien given to an unpaid supplier of labor and/or materials, and enables him to look to the property to which he supplied his labor or materials as a means of satisfying the debt.

If the ABC Construction Company does a remodeling job for Mr. Smith on his home at 118 Maple St., and Smith does not pay, ABC Construction Co. is considered to have a lien against the specific property—118 Maple St. Depending on particular state law, they may (if they comply with the statutory requirements) later institute proceedings to have the property sold, and have the debt satisfied out of the proceeds of the sale.

This seems to be an equitable way of assuring that suppliers will be paid. The problems arise, however, because of the time period given the supplier to file his lien claim, during which period the property might have been transferred to one who knows nothing of the unpaid debt. In the case of new construction, the likelihood of there being an unpaid supplier is greatest, since there are usually a substantial number of suppliers of labor and materials.

Let us suppose the XYZ Realty Development Company sells a lot and newly built home to Mr. Martin. The house was completed on June 10th, and title transferred on June 15th. One supplier of material, the City Lumber Company, is still owed $1,000 for lumber supplied to that job, and Martin is unaware of that fact. Of course, City Lumber could simply sue XYZ on the unpaid debt, but the ability to establish a lien against the property gives them additional assurance of being paid, particularly if XYZ is in poor financial condition.

Mr. Martin's problem may arise because, although when he took title June 15th, no lien claim was on record, City Lumber has a length of time, after furnishing material, to file a lien claim. For example, in North Carolina a supplier has 120 days after last furnishing his labor or material, within which to file his claim of lien. (He must also commence a lawsuit on the debt within 180 days, in order to be able to enforce the lien).

If City Lumber had last furnished lumber on, say, May 20, they would have until late in September to file a lien claim. Martin could find, three months after receiving a clear title, that his property now has a lien against it for $1,000.

There are ways by which a buyer may attempt to protect himself against this situation, but the technicalities of mechanic's liens are beyond the scope of our discussion. What is important is to understand the potential danger of a situation where substantial improvements have been made to property within a recent period. With this in mind, a potential buyer can investigate alternate means of protection.

General Liens. Unlike a specific lien, a general lien affects any property owned by the debtor. The most common example is a judgment.

Judgment: A court determination, usually awarding money to the successful party. When a lawsuit is instituted, the complaining party (plaintiff) typically is asking the court to decide that the party against whom the complaint is brought (defendant) should be required to pay a certain amount to the plaintiff. The nature of the suit is immaterial. If a judgment is obtained by plaintiff, this judgment is then docketed (entered into the record book).

When a judgment is docketed, it becomes a lien against any real property in the county owned by the judgment debtor. It is thus a general lien. It even constitutes a lien against property in the county later acquired by the debtor (in many states).

What if the judgment debtor owns no property in the county where the judgment was obtained and docketed, but he does own property in another county within the state? Generally state laws provide for filing the judgment in the second county so as to affect the property located there.

The period for which a judgment remains effective depends upon the law of the particular state. In most states, it is effective for 10 years, and in some states the period may be extended by bringing a new suit on the judgment before the expiration of the period.

If property is held by husband and wife as tenants by the entirety (the special husband-wife ownership, with right of survivorship we discussed in a previous chapter) a judgment against one of them will not create a lien against the property; for such lien to be created, the judgment must be against them both.

Judgments are enforced by *execution,* which consists of the issuance of a writ to the sheriff directing him to seize and sell the property.

Some states have a homestead exemption, which exempts from judgment creditors the property used as a homestead. Depending on the particular state, the amount of the exemptions may vary. In North Carolina, for example, the exemption is limited to a maximum of $1,000 and even there does not apply against tax or mechanic's liens, or mortgage debt incurred in the purchase of the property.

Decedent's Debts. One who has died is called a decedent. His debts are general liens against any property he owned at death. The usual procedure is to look to his personal property first, and then, if not sufficient to satisfy the debts, his real property may be reached.

This points out the necessity for particular care when property is being purchased from an estate, to be certain that there remain no outstanding debts of the estate which might constitute a lien against the property being purchased.

Where there is more than one lien on record against a debtor, their order of priority is generally determined by the respective dates they were filed or recorded. In the event of a foreclosure and sale of property, the amount realized would have to go to the holder of the lien with the earliest filing date. The remainder of the funds, if any, would then go toward satisfying the lien with the next oldest date of filing, and so on.

The liens we have discussed, as well as other claims we touched on briefly in earlier chapters, constitute "encumbrances" or clouds on the title. You will recall that we described a clear or marketable title as one that is free of such clouds. It is appropriate at this point, therefore, to discuss title insurance, a type of protection against clouds on title.

We think of insurance generally as compensation for loss caused by some future event. But title insurance is different in that it protects against something that may have taken place in the past, but is unknown to us.

A title insurance policy protects a purchaser of property against financial loss caused by some encumbrance or defect in the title of the property, which was unknown to him at the time of purchase. Of course, if a title search turns up some defect or encumbrance in the record, it will be excluded from coverage; a policy may be issued with certain exceptions or exclusions specified.

Policies are available not only from general insurers who offer this type of coverage, but from specialized title insurance companies. The applicant pays a one-time premium at the time of title closing, and he is thereafter covered for as long as he and his heirs own the property. The premium cost will vary regionally; for, let us say, a $35,000 house it could probably range from $75 to $200.

In addition to compensating an owner for loss because of some claim or encumbrance, the insurance company is obligated to defend the owner in any legal action arising out of such claim. This is important because, without title insurance, an owner would have the trouble and expense of defending even a groundless lawsuit or one based upon some claim later held to be invalid.

What we have described is an *owner's* title insurance policy. But even where the buyer of property does not obtain such a policy, if he is obtaining a mortgage loan with which to buy the property, the lending institution will probably require such a policy for its own protection, the cost of which must be borne by the buyer.

You may well ask, then, if title insurance is being issued for the mortgagee's protection, why should an owner obtain his own policy, since the insurance company will have to defend a claim and make good any loss?

The answer lies in the fact that the mortgagee's policy is to insure only his interest, which not only is less than the total value of the property, but is constantly diminishing, and eventually will cease to exist altogether, at which time the policy will terminate.

To illustrate, let us suppose that after a certain number of years of ownership, Mr. Jones finds his title in doubt because of some claim. The mortgage on his $35,000 property is now down to $5,000, and this is the only amount the mortgagee is concerned about. If the title insurance company should decide to pay the mortgagee the $5,000 rather than contest the claim, the owner would be left to defend the claim and possibly suffer whatever ultimate financial loss might develop, should his title be found to be defective.

Some title insurance companies, in situations where a mortgagee's policy is being issued, will issue an owner's policy for a small additional fee. In such case, since the buyer undoubtedly is paying for the mortgagee's policy, he would certainly be well advised to obtain protection for himself at small additional cost.

Lawyers Title Insurance Corporation
Home Office ~ Richmond, Virginia

JOINT PROTECTION POLICY OF TITLE INSURANCE

SCHEDULE A

1.

AMOUNT

$15,000.00

2.

INSURED

John Smith and Mary Smith and ABC Mortgage Company

3. On June 1 1971, at 10 o'clock, a. m., the title to the insured property is vested in:

4.

John Smith and Mary Smith

herein referred to as "vestee(s)".

5.

The land referred to in this policy is described as follows:

All that certain lot, piece or parcel of land situate in Henrico County, Virginia and shown as Lot 10, Block 6 on the Plan of Jonesboro, a plat of which is recorded in the Clerk's Office of the Circuit Court of Henrico County, Virginia in Plat Book 5, Page 72.

BEING the same property conveyed to John Smith and Mary Smith by deed from Jonesboro Development Corporation, dated May 20, 1964, filed for record May 22, 1964, Deed Book 67, Page 18, Clerk's Office, Circuit Court, Henrico County, Virginia.

6.

Countersigned:
The Title Insurance Agency

SPECIMEN COPY

Authorized Officer or Agent

7.

Issued at: Richmond, Virginia

8. File No. 12345
Page 1 of Sched. A-Pol No.

Form 54 Sched. A Rev. 9 67 - Litho in U.S.A.   **ORIGINAL - ISSUED IN DUPLICATE**   Joint Protection Policy

Lawyers Title Insurance Corporation
Home Office ~ Richmond , Virginia

JOINT PROTECTION POLICY OF TITLE INSURANCE

SCHEDULE B

Defects, liens, encumbrances and other matters, to which title insured by this Policy is subject.

1. Taxes for the year 1971 and subsequent years.

2. Restrictions appearing of record, copy attached. This policy insures the owner of the indebtedness that said restrictions have not been violated and that a violation thereof will not cause a forfeiture or reversion of title.

3. Reservation of easements for utility installation and maintenance affecting the rear five feet of insured premises, as contained in the restrictions.

4. As to the vestees: Any lien, or right to a lien, for services, labor or material heretofore or hereafter furnished, imposed by law and not shown by the public records.

5. Deed of trust from John Smith and Mary Smith, his wife, to K. D. Jones, Trustee, dated May 20, 1971, filed for record May 22, 1971, Deed Book 67, Page 20, to secure $10,000.00

Page 1 of Sched B—Pol. No.

Pol. Form 54 Sched. B Rev. 9-67 - Litho in U.S.A.   **ORIGINAL - ISSUED IN DUPLICATE**   Joint Protection Policy

6.

TAXES AND ASSESSMENTS

Real property taxes, imposed primarily at the county and local level, constitute an important means by which government can afford to operate, including public services such as schools, police and fire departments, streets and parks, etc. Although the property tax accounts for a smaller proportion of total government revenue than in years gone by, nevertheless the total dollar amount of real property taxes increases annually.

Property taxes are based on an "ad valorem" system, which simply means "according to value." Each parcel of real estate in the taxing area must be appraised in order to arrive at its market value. Against this figure is applied the percentage of market value that is either required by law or agreed upon in the particular area. For example, a parcel may have a market value of $25,000, and the property in that area is assessed at 60% of market value. This would make the *assessed valuation* of that parcel $15,000. Against this assessed valuation, the *tax rate,* whatever that might be, would be applied in order to compute the tax due.

How is this tax rate determined? Assume the tax district is a county. That county would first arrive at a budget for the forthcoming fiscal year. This is the amount of money it anticipates it will need, and which must therefore be raised. From this figure is subtracted money which will be obtained from sources other than real property taxation. The remainder is the sum which the real property in the county must produce in revenue. Dividing the total assessed valuation of all property in the county by the amount to be raised will give us the rate of taxation.

For example, suppose the Doakes County budget called for $10,000,000, of which $2,000,000 is expected to be raised by tolls, fines, license fees, etc., leaving $8,000,000 which must come from real property taxation. If the assessed valuation of all real property in Doakes County is $160,000,000 the tax rate would be:

$$\frac{\$\ 8,000,000}{\$160,000,000} = .05 \text{ or } 5¢ \text{ per dollar, or } \$5 \text{ per } \$100$$

Tax rates are generally expressed in number of dollars of tax per $100 of assessed valuation. In our example we would say that the tax rate is $5.

Sometimes tax rates are expressed in *mills* rather than dollars. A mill is one-tenth of a cent, and expressing the tax rate in mills gives us the rate per *dollar* of assessed valuation.

To repeat—a tax rate expressed in dollars gives us the rate per hundred dollars of assessed valuation. A rate expressed in mills gives us the rate per dollar.

In our example, we could express the tax rate as ''$5.'' or ''50 mills.''

You now should understand why, in comparing the tax burden of two different property owners, it is necessary to know more than just the assessed valuation. If Mr. Brown and Mr. Green own virtually identical homes in different towns, and Mr. Brown complains that his property is assessed for $30,000 while his friend Mr. Green's assessment figure is $25,000, we cannot automatically sympathize with Brown. To know what the true tax burden is for each of them, we must apply the tax rate; if the rate in Brown's town is $2 and Green's is $2.50, our sympathy for Brown would have been misplaced, since his tax is $600 per year and Green's is $612.50!

It is possible for a property owner to contest the amount of his assessed valuation by filing a notice of protest with the appropriate office. His protest will be heard, typically, by a board of review. Even where the board finds against him, the taxpayer may still carry the protest further by going to the courts, on the theory that the tax officials have proceeded in a manner contrary to the principles of law under which they operate.

In certain instances, property may be exempt from taxation, either partially or wholly. Some typical examples might be educational or religious institutions, hospitals, and property owned by the state or federal governments. Some states grant exemptions up to a stated amount or percentage for homes owned by war veterans or by ''senior citizens.'' In some cases, localities seeking to attract industry often have granted real property tax exemption for a period of time to a firm that will erect a plant, thus providing employment for a substantial number of the populace.

Special assessments should be distinguished from the real property tax. These assessments are one-time charges against property arising from some local improvement benefitting the property. If a roadway is paved, the individual parcels of real property on that street will benefit, and therefore the cost of the improvement is divided among them, in proportion to the degree of benefit for each. The structures on the respective parcels are not considered, since it is the land that is considered to have benefited and the amount of frontage in each parcel will determine its proportion of the assessment. (This does not automatically mean that lots will be assessed according to their value; corner lots traditionally are considered more valuable than lots in the middle of the block, yet would not be assessed on a higher basis.)

The initiative for a particular improvement may originate with a governmental body such as a city or town council, or it may come about through a petition from the property owners themselves who wish the improvement, and are willing to share the cost of it.

In many areas, where an assessment exceeds a certain dollar amount, the property owner has the option of paying it off in annual installments over a period of years. Usually each installment will include a low rate of interest on the remaining balance.

Assessments, like property taxes, become liens against the property, usually at the time they are fixed. Failure to pay the assessment renders the property liable for the payment as in the case of any other lien. Where installment payments are provided for, the law usually provides for such action upon default in the payment of any installment.

7.

LANDLORD AND TENANT

In our first chapter discussion of estates in land we pointed out the difference between freehold and non-freehold estates.

A non-freehold estate (sometimes called "less than freehold") is a *leasehold,* an estate not of ownership, but one in which a person occupies real property belonging to another, with his permission, for a period of time. At the end of that time, it is contemplated that the owner will get back possession of the property.

We commonly refer to the owner as the landlord, and the one to whom possession is given as the tenant. Their relationship arises from a contractual agreement between them called a lease. The technical designation for the parties is *lessor* (not "leasor") for the landlord, and *lessee* (not "leasee") for the tenant.

Must this lease be in writing? The answer depends on the length of the lease term and the law of the particular state. In most states a lease for more than one year must be in writing to be enforceable, but other states specify different periods. In North Carolina, for example, the lease must be in writing only if the term exceeds three years.

A word of caution—when we speak of a requirement that a particular agreement be in writing, we do not mean that if it is oral it is illegal; we simply mean that it would not be enforceable in a court of law, and therefore a party seeking to hold another to the agreement would find himself in the same position as if he had no agreement.

Even where the lease term is such that an oral lease would be valid and enforceable, our earlier warning to reduce all agreements to writing still applies. This will eliminate, or substantially reduce, the likelihood of misunderstanding, honest or otherwise.

A lease is a contract, and must therefore conform to the basic requirements for any contract, as we pointed out in an early chapter (legal capacity of the parties, a legal object, consideration, etc.).

The consideration for the use of the property is called *rent,* which may be payable in money, goods or services. The amount is usually set forth as a fixed dollar figure, but it need not be, so long as the rent is *determinable*. For example, if the rent called for in a store lease is 5% of the tenant's gross sales, this is not a *fixed* dollar amount, but it is *determinable* (at the end of the month).

Interestingly, if a lease for a term sets forth the total rent for the term, without specifying any intervals of payment, the entire amount is due and payable at the end of the term.

The four types of leasehold estates (tenancies) are the following:

Tenancy for Years. This is an estate for a stated term. It continues for a definite period of time, and ends at a specific time. Although called "tenancy for years," it need not be for years; it may be for a specific number of days, weeks, or months.

Tenancy from Year to Year (Periodic Tenancy). Here the duration of the tenancy is not definite. It continues for an indefinite number of terms (year to year, or month to month, or week to week). It renews itself from period to period, unless either the lessor or lessee terminates by giving the other party notice. The time required for giving such notice depends on state law. North Carolina statutes provide that one month's notice is required to terminate a year-to-year tenancy, while for month-to-month or week-to-week tenancies, the periods are one week and two days respectively.

Tenancy at Will. A tenancy for no definite duration of time. It may be terminated by either party at any time without notice. Courts would probably give a tenant time to vacate the premises. In the case of a tenant at will on farm property, who had planted a crop, if the landlord terminates the tenancy when the crop is ready to be harvested, tenant would likely be allowed to harvest it.

Tenancy at Sufferance. This is the lowest of the estates we are considering. It occurs when a tenant who was in possession lawfully, remains in possession after the expiration of his lawful tenancy. He is thus a "holdover," but has no legal rights, since his remaining in possession is due only to the inaction of the landlord. He is not entitled to any notice to vacate, but some states have statutes calling for notice even in this situation.

You may well raise the question of the apparent contradiction between the periodic tenancy and the tenancy at sufferance. Assume a tenancy from year to year, and no notice of termination is given; by our previous definition, if the tenant remains, there is a renewal of the year-to-year tenancy. Yet does this not fit the situation we have just defined as tenancy at sufferance, which the landlord could terminate at any time?

The answer lies in whether the landlord acknowledges a lawful tenancy by accepting rent. If he does, then the renewal of the period tenancy is acknowledged; if no rent is offered and accepted, then the tenant remains only at the "sufferance" of the landlord.

Let us now consider a few of the most common types of leases.

The *gross lease* is one we probably are most familiar with. The rent is a fixed amount paid to the landlord, who pays taxes, insurance, and other expenses of property ownership.

The *net lease* is so named because the tenant pays taxes, insurance and operating expenses, and the rent paid to the landlord is therefore a net amount. In some cases, the tenant might also undertake to make the mortgage payments, in which case the lease would be called a *net-net lease*.

The *percentage lease,* used frequently in retail store leasing, provides for a rent based upon the lessee's gross sales volume. Usually there is a flat minimum amount called for, plus a percentage of sales over a certain amount.

Index lease: The rent is tied to a specific index such as the Consumer Price Index; it will vary as the index moves up or down.

Graduated lease: This lease provides for systematic increases in rent at certain intervals during the lease term. This might be of particular value where the lessee is embarking on a new business venture.

Ground lease: Here the lease is for the "ground"—unimproved land. This is usually part of an agreement calling for the erection of a building by the tenant. Since the building will become part of the real property, some contractual arrangement must be made for the tenant to get back his cost, perhaps through the landlord eventually paying tenant for the building.

Sale and leaseback: This is a device of relatively recent origin that many businesses have found advantageous, primarily as a means of making available capital funds for internal use. Let us assume the X Mfg. Co. owns the property where its business is located. It sells this property to Z and simultaneously enters into a lease with Z. X, formerly the owner, now becomes a tenant, usually under a long-term lease.

X has now obtained cash which it can use in its operations. In addition, its rent payments, which reduce its taxable income, might constitute a tax advantage. (This would depend, of course, on comparing this with the advantage of tax-deductible mortgage loan interest, which it now would not have.)

Z now has the benefit of an income-producing property. Taxwise, it now also has the benefit of starting a fresh depreciation computation for the property.

Questions often arise with regard to the fitness of property for a particular use, and the obligation to make repairs. These matters may properly be the subject of an agreement between the landlord and the tenant, spelled out in the lease. But what if there is no specific agreement on these questions? Generally, there is no implied promise by the land-lord that property is fit for any particular purpose or use. In the case of a dwelling, of course, there is the implied warranty that the premises are fit for human habitation. But in a commercial lease situation, if a tenant leases property for the purpose of manufacturing widgets, and later finds that the flooring is not substantial enough to support the needed machin-ery, he cannot avoid the lease obligation on the ground that there has been a breach of warranty by the landlord.

A similar situation exists regarding repairs to the property. There is a general misconception that landlords are obligated to make all repairs to leased property, but this is not the case. Generally, leases provide that the tenant is to maintain the premises in good repair and upon expiration of the lease term is to return the premises in the same condition as when he entered upon his tenancy, except for normal ''wear and tear.'' The tenant is therefore under a duty to make ordinary repairs, unless the lease provides otherwise.

Some states, in the interest of ''consumer protection'' have enacted legislation requiring landlords to make necessary repairs to rented hous-ing.

At common law, destruction of the premises did not relieve the tenant of his lease obligation, but state laws have changed this so that the typical statute in most states provides that destruction terminates the lease, thereby relieving the tenant of further liability. In North Carolina, not even total destruction is required; there the statute provides that if the use of a building was the chief reason for the lease, and it is damaged to the extent that the cost to render it fit for use again would exceed the amount of one year's rent, the tenant may cancel the lease.

What happens to the tenant if the landlord sells the property? The lease remains in full force and effect, and the buyer of the property takes it subject to the lease.

In the case of a mortgage of the property, the tenant may or may not be affected. The question hinges on when the mortgage was recorded.

Suppose a lease is entered into in September, 1977, and in January, 1978 the landlord mortgages the property. The tenant's rights under the lease are protected and the mortgagee cannot terminate the lease even if there is a foreclosure proceeding.

If, however, when the lease was executed in September, 1977, there was already a mortgage of the property on record, the lease would be subordinate to the mortgage; in such case, a later default by the landlord and a foreclosure by the mortgagee could terminate the tenant's lease, so long as the tenant is made a party to the legal proceedings.

Here again, we see an illustration of the importance of recording instruments affecting real property. With some exceptions, the general rule applies—''first in time is first in right''—(time of *recording,* not execution).

It is quite common, particularly in commercial property, for an owner who is leasing space to another to insert in the lease a "subordination clause," providing that the tenant agrees that his lease rights will be subordinated to the rights of any subsequent mortgagee. This will make a later mortgage loan more easily available to the owner, since a lender's rights in the property would thereby be superior to the rights of the tenant under the law.

If property is taken by the public authorities under the right of eminent domain, any leases are terminated, but the tenant is entitled to an award for the value of the remaining unexpired term of his lease. The tenant must file and prove his claim. In order to avoid legal disputes, leases will usually contain a clause explicitly providing either for compensation to the tenant or for the landlord to receive the total of any condemnation award.

Just as the landlord has the right to transfer or mortgage his interest in the property, so, too, does the tenant have the right to *assign* or *sublet* his interest. There is a difference, however, between assignment and subletting. In an assignment, the tenant is transferring the entire balance of the lease term, and the new tenant stands in place of the original tenant. To illustrate, if L the landlord and T the Tenant have a lease agreement, and T assigns his lease to B, L and B are now parties to the lease agreement.

On the other hand, if T sublets to B, T is still L's tenant; B is really a subtenant of T for a limited time, at the end of which T goes back into possession. In a sublease, the subtenant and the landlord have no legal relationship.

Of course, for a tenant to assign or sublet, there must be no prohibition against such acton in his lease. Most leases provide that for an assignment or sublease, the consent of the landlord must be obtained. In the absence of such prohibition, the tenant is free to do either.

Even where the tenant properly assigns or sublets, he remains legally liable to the landlord, unless released by the landlord.

We have already mentioned some examples of a lease being terminated (destruction of the property, condemnation under eminent domain, giving of proper notice under certain tenancies) but there are others. If one party to a lease violates a provision of the lease (a breach of a condition) this generally gives the other party the right to treat the lease as terminated. The innocent party would then have the right to pursue whatever legal remedy is available to compensate him for any loss.

For example, if a tenant breaches the lease by failing to pay rent, the landlord may not only act to *evict* the tenant (oust him from possession) but may sue him for the amount of unpaid rent.

We should take note of the fact that eviction may be either *actual,* where action is taken to physically dispossess the tenant, or *constructive;* constructive eviction takes place when the conduct of the landlord creates a situation that renders the premises unfit to be tenanted. For example, if a dwelling is so infested with vermin that it is uninhabitable, this would constitute constructive eviction.

Again, we have before us an illustration of the difference between the *power* to do something and the *right* to do it. It may be within the power of either the landlord or the tenant to effectively terminate a lease; but if the termination is wrongful (i.e., a breach of a lease condition) the party terminating may be liable to the other for any loss caused by the termination.

8.

TITLE CLOSING

The "closing" of title refers to the time at which the title to property will pass from seller to buyer. This will be done by delivery of a deed, the payment of whatever amount is required of the buyer, and the execution and delivery of any other necessary documents. These matters can usually all be completed simultaneously at a meeting attended by the buyer and seller, their attorneys, a representative from the lending institution (if one is involved) and the real estate broker. The broker is not a party to the transaction, but he is there not only because of his commission which is involved, but to be of assistance, perhaps in furnishing information. In some areas he is responsible for preparing and distributing the "closing statement," the details of which we will go into later in this chapter.

Picture yourself as the seller of a $35,000 home to Mr. and Mrs. Phillips. It is quite likely that the Phillips gave an earnest money deposit to the broker at the time they first signed the contract. Let us say this deposit was $3500. At the closing, you expect this deposit to be turned over to you, plus the additional $31,500. (Of course, as we will see later, there will be some adjustments, as well as the broker's commission you will have to pay.) Now let us assume that you still have a mortgage on the property which has been reduced over the years to where the outstanding balance is now $19,000. If the Phillips are arranging their own financing, you will have to clear off this $19,000 mortgage so that you can deliver the property free and clear; you will do this at the closing by using part of the money the Phillips give you to pay off your $19,000 mortgage balance. In some areas, a representative of your mortgagee will participate in the closing because of this payoff. In other areas, an attorney is designated by all parties to handle the closing for all concerned, and to remit to the proper parties whatever payments are due them.

Of course, if the Phillips are "assuming" your mortgage, no payoff of the $19,000 is needed; the Phillips would simply take over this obligation as part of the $35,000 purchase price.

As seller, you will be expected to come to the closing with certain documents. First and foremost is the deed, which should contain the acknowledgment (so that it may be recorded).

You will be required to furnish documents showing that any liens or mortgages have been discharged. If there is a possibility that suppliers of labor or materials have not been paid, you should have signed receipts for payments from such suppliers. (This potential danger was pointed out in the section on mechanic's liens.)

If the buyer is taking over your property insurance, your policy, together with the completed assignment form, will be needed at the closing.

In areas where termites are a factor, you will furnish a certificate of termite inspection from a licensed exterminator. This certificate states that there are not termites present (or that termite-proofing has been done). The cost of this is borne by the seller. If the buyer is obtaining a VA, FHA, or Farm Home Loan, a termite inspection is required by their respective regulations.

If you are selling to the buyer any personal property in addition to the real property (for example, your draperies, a rug, etc.) a bill of sale will be needed. (A bill of sale does for personal property what a deed does for real property; it transfers title).

You will also need your most recent receipts showing that you have paid property taxes, water or sewer charges, and any assessments.

You will probably have to sign an affidavit of title at the closing. Since the closing takes place some time after the actual title search, it is possible that events affecting title could have taken place during that period. The affidavit of title is a statement under oath attesting to the fact that no bankruptcy or divorce proceedings have taken place, and that no judgments have been entered against you.

The buyer will have his own responsibilities at the closing. Primarily, his will be the obligation to have sufficient funds, not only to cover the purchase of the property, but also for what are called *closing costs*. This phrase refers to various items of disbursement—fees and charges, etc.— which are not part of the purchase price, but which must be paid for at the closing. Not all but most of these are borne by the buyer, although they may be the subject of individual negotiation between the parties. General custom, or the law, in a particular locality may also determine who pays a particular charge. The contract of sale should specify, as far as practicable, which costs are to be paid by each party.

Some typical charges which a buyer customarily pays are the following:

Title Insurance. If required by the lending institution, the buyer pays. Of course, an owner's policy, if desired, would be the buyer's responsibility.

Loan Assumption Fee. If the buyer is assuming the seller's mortgage, the mortgagee probably will charge a fee for transferring the loan.

Mortgage Origination Fee. Most lenders will charge a fee just for making the loan.

Survey. If a new survey is needed by the lender (or if the buyer merely wishes to have one).

Appraisal Fee. Usually the lender requires that an appraisal of the property be made in order to determine whether, and how much, to lend.

Legal Fee for Title Search. This will be required for the lender to obtain his title insurance (as well as an owner's policy, if one is required).

In the typical home-purchase situation, where a buyer is obtaining a mortgage loan for perhaps 90% of the purchase price, he should be aware that his closing costs may total about 3% of the loan amount, as a general rule of thumb.

The seller will customarily have to shoulder certain charges such as legal fees for the preparation of the deed and any other legal work necessary for the seller to be able to furnish a clear and marketable title.

Most states impose a tax on the transfer of real property which is paid through the purchase of a tax stamp. The stamp is then affixed to the deed. This tax, generally the obligation of the seller, is a nominal amount based upon the selling price of the property. In North Carolina, as in some other states, the tax is 50¢ per $500 or fraction thereof. (Generally, if part of the purchase price consists of a mortgage assumption by the buyer, this amount is not included in the tax computation; the tax is paid only on the "fresh money" in the price.)

So far we have considered items of expenditure that are the responsibility of either the buyer or the seller alone. But there are some items which might involve both these parties because the payment for the item covers a period of time during which the seller and buyer each was the owner for a portion of that period. For example, suppose on January 1 the seller paid his real property tax of $300 for the succeeding year. He then sells his property by transferring title to the buyer on July 1. Should not the buyer be responsible for taxes after July 1? Certainly, but the only way to accomplish this is for the buyer to reimburse the seller at the closing in an amount equal to the proportion of the $300 tax covering the period from July 1 to the end of the year.

This procedure is called *proration,* and we will go into this in greater detail in our discussion of closing statements. (Proration is nothing more than apportioning between buyer and seller certain items of expenditure, so that each will pay his share covering the period during which he was the owner of the property.)

CLOSING STATEMENTS

A closing statement is an itemized account of all the financial aspects of the title closing. The buyer's statement, when totalled, will show the "balance due from buyer;" the seller's statement will show the "balance due to seller." In addition, there is generally prepared a *broker's resume statement,* which details and accounts for any funds received and/or disbursed by the broker.

The closing statement shows what took place at the closing, yet is prepared in advance. This may seem contradictory, but is necessary both because of the time-consuming computations involved, and because the parties must be prepared in advance for what will be required financially at the closing.

The statement is on a form with lines for the individual items to be described and the dollar amounts to be entered either in a "debit" or "credit" column as shown below. (A separate statement is prepared for buyer and seller.)

ITEM	DEBIT	CREDIT

First, let us make clear what the words "debit" and "credit" indicate. A debit is a charge that is being made, something that will reduce one's funds. If it is a charge to the seller, it will reduce the funds he is to receive at the closing; if it is a charge to the buyer, it will reduce his funds by increasing the amount he will have to produce at the closing.

Conversely, a credit is something that will add to one's funds. A credit to the seller will increase his funds by adding to the amount he will be entitled to receive; a credit to the buyer will add to his funds by reducing the amount he will have to produce.

Financial items of the closing transaction can be divided into two broad categories:

1. Those involving an exchange of value between buyer and seller.
2. Those involving an expenditure by either buyer or seller to some third party.

Let us consider the first category. An exchange of value between buyer and seller simply means that the item constitutes something for which one of the parties will pay the other. An obvious example is the purchase price of the property, let us say, $30,000. This item will be paid by the buyer to the seller—therefore, a charge or "debit" to the buyer, and a "credit" to the seller. It would be shown as follows: (for simplification, we will put the buyer's and seller's statements together, although they are properly separate accounts).

	BUYER		SELLER	
	Debit	Credit	Debit	Credit
Purchase Price	$30,000			$30,000

Suppose there was an article of personal property to be included in the transaction, but shown separate from the real property—draperies, for example. If the price was $200, there would be the following entry shown:

	BUYER		SELLER	
	Debit	Credit	Debit	Credit
Draperies	$200			$200

It should be apparent to you by now that, with regard to items representing an exchange of value between buyer and seller, a debit to one party must be a credit to the other. One party's expenditure is the other party's income. (Caution: This rule applies only to the "exchange of value" items; as we shall see, it does not apply where a party is charged for an expenditure that is going to a third party.)

We referred earlier to prorated items. These involve both parties, and will therefore result in debiting one and crediting the other, but our problem now is to learn how to apportion the item properly.

Let us use property taxes as an example. In some areas these taxes are paid in advance for a year; in other areas they are paid at the end of the year, and cover the preceding year. In some cities or counties, they are payable semi-annually.

If we suppose a situation in which the property taxes amount to $360 payable December 31 for the preceding year, and there is a title closing on June 15th, we will have to prorate the tax item; the seller is responsible for taxes during his period of ownership (January 1 to June 15); the buyer is responsible for his period of ownership (June 15 to December 31).

Generally, prorating is done on the basis of 30-day months, as though there are 360 days in the year (in large commercial and industrial transactions, actual days are computed, since the effect on the total amount might be substantial).

In our example, the $360 annual tax amounts to $30 per month, or $1 per day. Since the seller owned the property for a period of 5 months and 15 days (January 1 to June 15) he is responsible for $165 of the total tax figure; without any separate calculation, we know that the buyer must be responsible for the balance—$195.

Now, how do we enter this in our closing statement? Remember that in items representing an exchange of value between buyer and seller, you cannot debit both parties or credit both parties; a debit to one is a credit to the other, and the dollar amount must be the same.

The key lies in the answer to the question: "Which party has paid (or will pay) the total of the item?" In our example, since the tax will be due December 31st, the buyer will pay the $360 at that time. Since our calculations showed that the seller is responsible for $165 of this, we should now have our statement show that we are charging the seller this amount and reimbursing the buyer accordingly. We therefore debit the seller and credit the buyer thus:

| | BUYER | | SELLER | |
	Debit	Credit	Debit	Credit
Real Property Tax		$165	$165	

Suppose the tax payment time in that area had been January 1 for the succeeding year? In that case, the seller would have paid the $360 in advance, and we would then simply reverse our procedure by debiting the buyer for *his* share ($195) and crediting the seller with that amount.

In some areas it is customary to use actual days rather than 30-day months, even in smaller transactions involving residential property. In such case the amount of the item would be divided by 365 to obtain the daily rate; the actual number of days from January 1 would then be computed.

For example, assume a tax item of $420 and a closing date of March 18th.

$$\frac{420}{365} = \$1.15 \text{ per day}$$

January	31 days
February	28 days
March	18 days
Total	77 days

$$77 \times \$1.15 = \$88.55$$

Here the seller's obligation is for $88.55. If he had paid the tax in advance, buyer would be debited $331.45 ($420 less $88.55) and seller would be credited with that amount.

If the tax, instead of being due at the beginning of the year, is due at the end of the year, then buyer will be paying the entire $420 at that time; we would therefore debit seller $88.55 and credit buyer with that same amount.

Obviously, in prorating the property tax, the time when the tax is due will determine whether the buyer owes the seller, or vice versa.

In prorating a prepaid fire insurance policy, the same computation is followed. Since it is a prepaid item, the buyer will always be debited, since he will owe the seller for the unexpired remaining term of the policy (of course, insurance is an item only where the buyer is taking over the seller's policy).

Now that you have some idea as to how to handle the debit and credit of items involving an exchange of value between buyer and seller, the answer to the following question may come as a surprise.

If the buyer is assuming the seller's mortgage as part of the purchase price, how is this item shown?

If the mortgage being assumed is $19,000, here is the way that item would appear:

	BUYER		SELLER	
	Debit	Credit	Debit	Credit
Assumption of Mortgage		$19,000	$19,000	

How, you may ask, can the buyer be *credited* with an item that is an obligation he is assuming? The answer lies in our original definitions of debit and credit. Does the item increase or decrease one's funds? By assuming the $19,000 mortgage, the buyer is increasing his funds, since he is reducing the amount he will need at the closing. (If the purchase price is $35,000, he would need this amount for the closing; by assuming the mortgage he reduces the amount needed by $19,000).

Conversely, the explanation for debiting the seller is that his funds are reduced by $19,000, since, instead of receiving $35,000 at the closing, he will receive only $16,000.

Where the buyer is assuming the existing mortgage, there will be an item of accrued interest on this mortgage. If, for example, the closing date is June 15th, the interest on the mortgage for the month of June must be prorated. If as in most cases, the July 1 mortgage payment will include interest for June, then the buyer will be making the payment later, and the seller should be debited for the interest from June 1 to June 15th. If, on the other hand, the mortgage loan calls for interest payments in advance for the month, then the seller would have paid June's interest amount in his June 1st payment, and the buyer should be debited for the amount of interest from June 15th to July 1.

As in other buyer-seller items, the amount of the debit to one party is a credit to the other.

If buyer has given an earnest money deposit at the time of contract, this money, in all likelihood, was given to the broker to be held by him in escrow. Since this was, therefore, not a direct exchange of value between buyer and seller, this item is shown only as a credit to buyer (it reduces the amount buyer will need at the closing). It does not appear on the seller's statement since he did not receive the deposit. However, the item will appear on the broker's resume statement, as we shall see, since it is something for which he must account.

Turning to our second category of closing statement items—these involve items of expenditure by a party, but not paid to the other party. For example, the broker's commission is a debit to the seller (it will reduce his funds) but it is not shown at all on the buyer's statement (it did not increase his funds). On the other hand, an item such as an appraisal fee would be debited to buyer since he is responsible for this payment, but would not appear on seller's statement.

When the respective debit and credit columns are totalled, the smaller column total is subtracted from the larger; the result on the buyer's statement shows the "balance due from buyer;" the seller's statement will show the "balance due to seller." The following is a sample:

	BUYER'S STATEMENT		SELLER'S STATEMENT	
	Debit	Credit	Debit	Credit
Purchase price	$35,000			$35,000
Assumption of mortgage		19,000	19,000	
Accrued mortgage interest		64	64	
Insurance	140			140
Property taxes		280	280	
Tax stamps			35	
Attorney's fee for deed			25	
Title insurance	100			
Fee for recording deed	5			
Appraisal fee	75			
Earnest money deposit		3,500		
Broker's commission			1,750	
(For each statement, subtract smaller total from larger total)	$35,320	22,844	21,154	35,140
Balance due from buyer		12,476		
Balance due to seller			13,986	

Your first reaction might be to question why the "balance due from buyer" and "balance due to seller" are not the same amount; but remember—not all items constitute an exchange of value between buyer and seller. The broker's commission, for example, represents a debit to seller, but has nothing to do with the buyer.

The broker's commission, as well as other possible items, will show up in the broker's resume statement.

The broker's resume statement accounts for all funds which the broker has received and disbursed. A sample might look like this:

ITEM	DEBIT	CREDIT
Earnest money deposit	$ 3,000	
Check from buyer	9,335	
Total to account for	$12,335	
To pay seller's expenses		$ 90
To pay buyer's expenses		178
Broker's commission		2,800
Check to seller		9,267
Total accounted for		$12,335

As you can readily see, the extent of the broker's involvement in the financial mechanics of the closing depends largely on local practice.

9.

VALUATION AND APPRAISAL

To appraise something, whether real estate or anything else, is to offer an opinion as to its value. The problem arises as to what we define "value" to be. We hear of book value, market value, replacement value and other designations—even "sentimental" value.

For our purpose we are concerned primarily with *market value*. This may be defined as the price a rational buyer would pay to a rational seller, where neither party is acting under the pressure of unusual circumstances.

For market value to exist, four basic elements must be present, and the extent to which they are present will affect the market value of any given property. These elements are *utility, scarcity, demand,* and *transferability*. Let us briefly define each.

Utility: The degree to which a need is filled, or some service rendered. It may reflect material utility (monetary return) or psychological utility (pride or comforts of home ownership).

Scarcity: The so-called law of supply and demand. The degree to which property is or is not available will affect value.

Demand: What we really mean is *effective* demand—the needs or desires of individuals backed up by the economic ability to purchase.

Transferability: For property to have value, it must be freely transferable. If there are any circumstances which prevent A from being able to transfer good title to B, the property has no market value, regardless of any other factors of desirability.

Assuming that the above elements are present, to a greater or lesser degree, in any particular property, there are two other principles (out of many) that are especially meaningful.

The principle of *highest and best use* refers to that use of property which is calculated to produce the highest net return (either in monetary return or amenities). Property should be appraised at its highest and best use.

The *substitution* principle means that the value of property cannot exceed the cost of its replacement. If there is a home available, for example, that is substitutable for the one we are evaluating, and is available for $2,000 less, our valuation figure will likely drop by that amount.

Before an appraisal of property can be undertaken, the purpose of the appraisal must be determined. This is so because, as we have already indicated, there are different kinds of "value." Thus, an appraisal for, let us say, insurance purposes would be concerned chiefly with replacement value, while an appraisal for purposes of sale would have "market value" in mind.

As a preliminary step to analyzing each of the three approaches to property appraisal, the following chart will be helpful in illustrating the overall plan:

THE APPRAISAL PROCESS

Identify Purpose of Appraisal

Collect Necessary Data

Apply Each of the Approaches to Value

Cost Approach	Market Data Approach	Income Approach
1. Separate land value	1. Obtain comparable sales figures	1. Compute annual gross income
2. Compute cost to reproduce building	2. Prepare individual comparisons with subject property, making necessary adjustments	2. Deduct for vacancies and collection losses, to obtain effective income
3. Deduct depreciation from (2)	3. Evaluate subject property	3. Deduct annual expenses, to obtain net income
4. Add back land value		4. Capitalize, to obtain value

Correlate the three estimates,
to arrive at appraisal value

While our discussion of appraisal will not be deeply comprehensive, we should understand at the outset that a competent, professional apprais-al involves using each of the three approaches shown on our chart; the respective results are then correlated (which we will go into later in the chapter) in order to arrive at our final evaluation.

You well may ask why there should be any differences in the final evaluation figure as between two or even three of the approaches. Re-member that measuring the "value" of property for, say, income-produc-ing purposes might not involve the same yardstick of measurement as property to be used solely for one's residence.

Market Data Approach

This is sometimes called the *comparative approach*. Basically, it involves comparing the subject property with similar properties that have been sold recently. Assuming that a sufficient number of such sales can be located, the method is a fairly reliable means of estimating what a property should bring in the market.

The method is simple and easy to apply, and is particularly useful for appraising single-family residential property. It depends, of course, on the availability of a number of similar sales; the greater the number of such sales, and the closer in time and similarity to the subject property, the more accurate our appraisal will be.

As our chart shows, the first step consists of obtaining comparable sales figures. Locating such "comparables" is not difficult, so long as there is a fairly active market in the type of property under consideration. If a broker is undertaking the appraisal, his own records might supply such comparables; in addition, he could call on his fellow-brokers in the community, as well as the local tax assessing office and lending institu-tions.

Naturally, we do not expect to find comparables that are identical with the subject property. But we would prefer to use those that are closest to the subject in characteristics and in time of sale. Any differences will be taken into account by adjusting our figures upward or downward.

Some basic rules in using comparable sales:

1. The comparable sale should be as recent as possible, preferably not over one year ago.

2. It should be one in which there are no personal or economic factors that would have distorted the price paid. For example, a transaction between close relatives, or a "distress" sale brought about by some unusual financial circumstances. (A foreclosure sale certainly would not represent a typical transfer for purposes of comparison.)

3. The comparable should be located in the same general area as the subject, and similar in physical characteristics.

What is done is to chart the various comparables for the different elements of value, and adjust either upward or downward, depending on whether our subject property benefits or suffers, on a comparative basis, with regard to each of the factors. For example, if a comparable has a one-car carport and the subject a two-car carport, we would adjust upward by the value of the additional carport area. (We always adjust *to* the subject property; if the particular characteristic has greater value in the subject, there will be a plus adjustment; if less value, the adjustment will be minus.)

Let us consider a sample table of adjustments:

	Comparable #1	Comparable #2	Comparable #3
Date of Sale	2 weeks ago	3 months ago	1 year ago
Selling Price	$40,000	$38,000	$35,000
Items of Adjustment:			
Time	0	+ $1500	+ $2500
Location	0	0	− $1000
Fireplace	0	0	+ $1100
Air Conditioning	− $1300	0	− $1300
Lot	0	0	0
Number of baths	+ $ 600	0	0
Net adjustments	− $700	+ $1500	+ $1300
Indicated value of subject:	$39,300	$39,500	$36,300

(These are only some of the adjustment items that might be involved.) A plus amount indicates that the subject is superior to the comparable; a minus indicates that the subject is inferior.

In the above table, for example, we have decided that during the passage of one year since comparable sale #3, realty values for a property such as this have increased by $2,500. The lot for each of the comparables apparently is not basically any different from the subject. As regards air-conditioning, which the subject does not have, this renders it $1,300 lower in value than comparables #1 and #3, but there is no change from comparable #2 which does not have air-conditioning.

As to number of baths, subject has the same number as comparables

#2 and #3, but has one bath more than comparable #1, hence the "+ $600."

If you refer back to our chart "The Appraisal Process," you will see that we have done what is described under the Market Data Approach (assuming that our list of adjustment items was complete).

How do we reconcile the disparity between the three comparables used? Simply by weighting each of them according to the degree of applicability. Comparable #3 has the most adjustments and is the least current; we would therefore give it a weight of perhaps 1. Since comparable #1 is the most current, we would probably give it a weight of perhaps 3, and give comparable #2 a weight of 2.

Adding these together, with their respective weights, would give us the following:

$$3(39,300) \quad + \; 2(39,500) \quad + \; 1(37,300)$$
$$\$117,900 \quad + \; \$79,000 \quad + \; \$37,300 \quad = \$234,200$$

Dividing this figure ($234,200) by the number of weighting units (6) gives $39,033, rounded off to $39,000.

The technique of adjusting consists of using a dollar value to indicate how much more or less a rational buyer would pay for the property because of the presence or absence of the particular item.

The Cost Approach

The cost approach to valuation involves estimating the amount that would be required to reproduce a property in its existing condition. Note the phrase "in its existing condition"; it is all very well to figure out the cost to reproduce a structure, but that would give us a *new structure* cost, and presumably our subject property is not new. Therefore, as we shall see, it becomes necessary to allow for depreciation.

The more recent the structure, the more accurate and appropriate the cost approach would be, since the depreciation factor would be less involved. The cost approach is also extremely useful where there is not an active market in the type of property being appraised. For example, if the subject were a hospital, the market data approach would be difficult to use, since comparable sales are few and far between.

The basic formula in the cost approach is:

$$V \quad = C \qquad - \qquad D$$
$$(\text{Value}) \quad = (\text{Replacement cost}) - (\text{Depreciation})$$

The first step in this approach is to estimate the value of the land. We do this because we will separate this figure, and hold it aside while we do our computations for the structure. The reason for this is that our structure computations will involve depreciation, and land does not depreciate.

A word of explanation: When we say that land does not depreciate, we do not mean that land values never decline. What we do mean is that, unlike a structure, land does not "wear out." Buildings have what is called an economic life—a normal period of usefulness—and thus are considered "wasting assets." Since land does not fall within this category, we do not include it in our overall computation; we will add the land value after completing our computation regarding the structure.

According to our chart, step #1 in the cost approach is to obtain the land value, and hold it aside. The market approach is used to obtain this information—comparable sales are utilized, and appropriate adjustments made, as described in the section on the market data approach. Remember that the principle of *highest and best use* controls; the valuation should be based on the highest and best use of the property even if that is not the use to which it is now being put.

Step #2 involves computing the cost to reproduce the building. Although there are three methods by which this may be done, we will consider only the simplest and most commonly used formula—the square foot method. This is done by taking the replacement cost per square foot (for the particular type and quality of construction in the subject property) and multiplying it by the number of square feet in the property. It should be noted that, in appraisal, the *outside* measurements of the structure are used.

To illustrate, if we are appraising a residential structure of 1500 square feet, and we determine that the replacement cost is $22 per square foot, our preliminary figure for step #2 would be $33,000.

Now, how do we arrive at the $22—the figure per square foot? Obviously, we must obtain building cost information. One way would be to obtain from local building contractors and suppliers the cost figures for the various components of the structure, but this method would be quite involved and cumbersome. There are organizations which publish construction cost information that is periodically up-dated, and available by annual subscription. In these publications certain basic description standards of construction are furnished; from these the appraiser can make adjustments upward or downward for features the subject property includes or lacks. The cost of the respective features, whether they be in structural components or built-in appliances, is given, so that the adjustments may be computed.

Construction costs in different regions of the country may deviate upward or downward from the standard cost. The publication service therefore provides a "local multiplier" to advise of local deviation from the standard. For example, since the standard is 100, if the local multiplier in your area is shown as 1.04, this would indicate that construction costs in that area are 104% of the standard (or 4% higher). On the other hand, if the local multiplier is .93, the construction costs would be 93% of the standard figure (or 7% less).

Assuming we have now completed step #2, the computation of the cost to reproduce the building, we now proceed to step #3. This involves computing accrued depreciation. Since our reproduction cost would be for a new building, we must make an adjustment to this figure to take into account the extent to which the building has been "used up" or "worn out."

As we pointed out earlier, a structure is a "wasting" asset, that is, it does wear out. In addition, there may have been other factors at work (economic or environmental, perhaps) that would tend to reduce the value of the structure.

All of these elements are lumped into what is called *depreciation*, which is simply the term used to describe a lessening of value, from whatever cause. The word "accrued" refers to the fact that it has already taken place, so that "accrued depreciation" describes the loss in value that has taken place from the time the structure was new until the present.

In order to compute depreciation, we must first understand that there are three types:

1. *Physical deterioration*. This refers to the degree of "worn-outness" of the structure, caused by the elements, wear and tear, etc.
2. *Functional obsolescence:* Loss in value caused by loss in usefulness. This could be caused by such things as poor room layout, inadequate closet space, inadequate electrical wiring, obsolete plumbing, etc.
3. *Economic obsolescence:* Here loss in value is caused by forces *external* to the structure, such as a change in the neighborhood caused by the presence of an industrial plant. Even a serious economic condition such as severe unemployment in the area would come within this definition.

To measure depreciation in terms of dollars, we might apply a straight-line depreciation technique. This assigns a "useful economic life" to the structure, let us say 50 years; we would then assume that the structure depreciates at a uniform rate of 2% each year. If the structure were one to which a normal economic life of 25 years had been assigned, a depreciation rate of 4% per year would apply. These economic life spans are, of course, arbitrary; they do not mean that at the end of the particular term the structure is expected to collapse. The Internal Revenue Service, for example, has published guidelines specifying recommended useful economic life figures for various types of structures.

The more accepted practice in measuring depreciation is to break it down into the three categories mentioned above, compute each separately, and then add the three figures together.

Let us measure physical depreciation. This type may consist of both *curable* and *incurable* items. Deterioration that results from "deferred maintenance" (failure to make ordinary needed repairs such as painting, replacing broken windows, etc.) would probably constitute curable deterioration. The measure of this would be the cost to cure it.

Incurable deterioration refers to a condition which it does not pay to remedy. If the cost to cure is greater than the increase in value that would result, it is considered *incurable* (from an economic standpoint). This condition usually results from the age of the structure and would refer to its basic components. Here we are dealing with a subjective concept of the appraiser—what is called the "effective age" of the structure, rather than the actual chronological age. It is possible, for example, for a 20-year-old building to be in such unusually good (or poor) condition that in the eyes of the appraiser, its *effective age* is 15 years (or, perhaps, 30 years).

The appraiser would then take the effective age and apply the ratio of depreciation against the reproduction cost. To illustrate, if a building with a useful economic life of 40 years is estimated to have an effective age of 30 years, and its reproduction cost is $60,000, the depreciation figure for incurable physical deterioration would be $45,000 (three-fourths of its economic life; or 2½% per year for 30 years).

It is true, of course, that the components of a building do not all wear out at a uniform rate, but to separate each such component and apply a rate of deterioration would be a staggering task.

So much for measuring physical deterioration. Turning to functional obsolescence, we apply the same standards. Curable functional obsolescence (a coal-burning furnace) would be measured by the cost to cure (convert the system to oil burner). To measure incurable functional obsolescence, however, we use a formula based on the loss of potential income. In residential property, we assume that the particular condition, say, poor design, would cause a decrease in rental value if the property were being rented. This is, of course, a subjective judgment. What is done is to obtain a selling price figure for comparables, and also a rental figure for comparables. The ratio between the two figures is called a *gross rent* multiplier.

To illustrate, if properties comparable to the subject have been sold for $30,000, and comparables have been renting for $200 per month, then they are selling for 150 times the rent. The gross rent multiplier is thus said to be 150. This multiplier is the means by which we "capitalize" the loss of rental income (to capitalize is to obtain a valuation amount from an income figure).

If the appraiser decides that the condition of functional obsolescence would reduce the rental income by $10 per month, he multiplies this $10 by the gross rent multiplier of 150, and the resulting figure, $1500, is the measure of incurable functional obsolescence.

Economic obsolescence, since it refers to external conditions, is generally considered to be incurable. We cannot, by spending money, alter some sever economic condition in the area, or the noise and exhaust fumes from a newly constructed interstate highway. For residential property we measure by using the gross-rent multiplier, as with functional obsolescence. However, note that economic obsolescence will affect both land and building; since, in step #1 of our cost approach we presumably used comparable land sales in the area affected by the economic obsolescence, the effect on the land has already been taken into account. We will therefore be concerned in our measurement only with that portion which applies to the building. If the building represents, for example, 80% of the total value of the property, then only 80% of our figure for economic obsolescence will apply.

Let us summarize what we have just discussed:

Measuring Depreciation

Physical Deterioration
    Curable: Cost to cure
    Incurable: Ratio between reproduction cost and effective age.

Functional Obsolescence
    Curable: Cost to cure
    Incurable: Capitalize estimated rental income lost (gross rent multiplier × estimated monthly rental loss).

Economic Obsolescence:
    Incurable: Capitalize as above, but separate land. Use only that proportion that building bears to total property value.

Sample computation based on cost approach to valuation:

Reproduction Cost:				$38,000
Less Depreciation:				
Physical Deterioration				
Curable	$ 800			
Incurable	3400			
		$4200		
Functional Obsolescence				
Curable	$ 400			
Incurable	900			
		1300		
Economic Obsolescence				
None		-0-		
Total Depreciation				5,500
Depreciated Cost of Improvements				$32,500
Estimated Land Value				4,000
			Total Value	$36,500

After measuring and totalling the types of depreciation, we have added back the land value obtained in step #1.

The Income Approach

The third of our approaches to valuation treats property on the basis of its income-producing capability. This is, of course, most appropriate to property that is now producing income, but it can be used for any type of property, since all property has such potential use.

If property will produce a stream of income over its remaining economic life, it is possible to translate this future income into a dollar amount of present value. What we do is to estimate the annual net income the property will produce, and then, by the "capitalization" process we referred to before, convert this income into a present value figure.

Step #1: Estimate annual potential gross income. This figure is the total annual income if the property were fully rented, and refers to what is called *economic rent* (the amount of rent the property would command in the open market). This figure may or may not be the same as the *contract rent* (the amount presently stipulated in a lease). In estimating this income, we consider the present and past income of the property as well as the income produced by comparable properties.

Step #2: Deduct an allowance for vacancies and uncollectable rents. Under normal circumstances, some vacancies will exist, and some rents will be lost through uncollectability. The loss experience of the past, as well as the neighborhood, type of tenants, etc. will largely determine the extent of this item. Subtracting this figure from the gross income will give us the *effective gross income.*

Step #3: Compute annual expenses and deduct this amount from effective gross income to obtain net income.

Annual expenses comprise three classifications. These are:

1. Fixed expenses, such as taxes and insurance.
2. Operating expenses, (variable) such as heat, utilities, janitorial, etc.
3. Reserve for replacement. Annual allowance set aside for items normally requiring replacement at predictable intervals (new roof, carpeting, etc.).

Step #4: Capitalize the net income into a statement of value. What we must do is establish the present value of future income. Expressed as a simple formula, the value would be stated as:

$$V \text{ (value)} = \frac{I \text{ (income)}}{R \text{ (rate)}}$$

If we divide the net income by the rate, we will establish value. The problem remaining is, then, to establish an applicable rate.

If you knew that Mr. Jones was receiving $2,000 annually in interest income on his deposit in a 6% savings account, you could readily compute the amount he had on deposit (the *value* of his principal). The question would be "6% of what amount would equal $2,000?" Now transfer those figures to a real estate situation: If there is property that returns a net income of $2,000 annually, and the going rate of return expected by investors is 6%, what is the value of the property? Using our formula:

$$\text{Value} = \frac{\text{Income ($2,000)}}{\text{Rate} \quad (.06)}$$

This would give us $33,333 as the value, which would mean that $33,333 would be the most an investor would pay for the property.

But the capitalization rate should include more than just the return on the investment; it should include provision for the return *of* the investment. In the case of the savings account, the depositor knows that in addition to his interest, he will also get back the amount of his deposit (the principal). The real estate investor should be able also to provide for the recapture of his original investment through an annual rate, which we will add to the basic capitalization rate. If, for example, the economic life of the property is 40 years, he would wish to add 2½% per year to the basic rate in order to provide for a return of his investment.

Additionally, the investor may wish a certain rate to compensate him for the risk involved in the investment. In our hypothetical example, we might end up with the following:

Interest rate	.06	
Recapture rate	.025	
Risk factor	.02	
Capitalization rate	.105	or 10½%

The alternative techniques by which land and building are separated and capitalization methods applied are beyond the scope of our discussion; but mention should be made of the fact that, in applying our basic principle in step #4, we must take into account that the annual income is a *future* stream. In obtaining present values of future income, we use mathematical tables in which these values are pre-determined.

To illustrate, $1,000 to be received two years from now does not have as high a present value as a $1,000 payment to be received one year from now. If the payment one year from now has a present value of $943, and the payment two years from now has a present value of $930, the present value of a two-year series of $1,000 payments would be $1,873.

A simple example under the income approach might be the following:

A 15-unit apartment building, each apartment renting for $200 per month, with a 10% vacancy experience:

Gross income:	15 × $200 × 12 months =	$36,000
Less vacancy factor:	(.10 × $36,000)	− 3,600
	Gross effective income	$32,400

Expenses:

Utilities	$1,000	
Insurance	500	
Taxes	1,800	
Replacement Reserve	1,200	
	————	
		4,500
Net annual income		$27,900

Capitalization rate:

Interest	8.5%
Risk factor	2.0%
Recapture	2.5%
	————
Capitalization rate	13.0%

Valuation:

$$V = \frac{Income}{Rate}$$

$$V = \frac{27,900}{.13}$$

$V = \$214,615$, rounded off to $214,600

Correlating the Three Approaches

After completing the three approaches to valuation, we must correlate them to arrive at the final evaluation figure. Correlation is *not* simply averaging the three; each approach must be weighted according to its applicability to the subject property. Income property would probably call for the greatest weight to be given to the income approach, while the market data approach would carry the greatest weight in single-family residential property.

There should not be a great divergence among the figures obtained by the three different approaches. Should those figures show a wide range, it would be well to check back for computation errors.

10.

LICENSING OF BROKERS AND SALESMEN

While there is no federal law regulating real estate brokerage activity as such, each state has its own law by which it requires licensing of real estate brokers and salesmen.

The requirements vary from state to state, but the basic purpose is to protect the public from those who, because of dishonesty or lack of capability, might engage in real estate activities that would cause great financial loss.

Real estate brokerage includes not only the selling, but the buying, leasing, exchanging or financing of property for another person. To engage in any of these activities would require licensing. There are certain exceptions; for example, to engage in any of these activities with regard to your own property does not require a license. Nor is a license required for persons acting under court appointment, such as executors under wills, and trustees in bankruptcy. Attorneys-at-law, when acting for clients, are permitted to handle real property, but almost all states require that an attorney who wishes to engage in real estate brokerage must obtain a broker's license.

The right to a license depends not only upon passing an examination but upon requirements of education and/or experience. Particular state regulations very widely, ranging from completion of a 30-hour approved course in Real Estate, to two years of experience as a licensed salesman plus completion of courses.

The salesman's license is usually obtained by successfully passing an examination, but the regulations generally provide that such license is valid only when the licensee is actively working for a licensed broker.

In the early days of licensing laws, 50 to 60 years ago, some such laws were challenged on constitutional grounds, the argument being that they violated the 14th Amendment by depriving citizens of the right to engage in a particular occupation of their choosing. In a situation where the wording of the law might be considered purely exclusionary, this argument would have some validity; in North Carolina, for example, the licensing law was rewritten and passed in 1957, and since then has successfully withstood the challenge to its constitutionality. Courts recognize today that the purpose of the licensing law is not simply to bar new entrants into the field, but to impose standards of competency on those seeking to enter. Since the state's police power gives it the right to act in the protection of the public's general welfare, such licensing legislation is amply justified.

Generally, licensing examinations test the knowledge of the applicant not only on general principles of real estate, but on the particular regulations of his or her state. These regulations are usually contained in two areas—the licensing law and the rules and regulations of the state real estate board or commission.

The North Carolina licensing law gives the state real estate board the power to adopt rules and regulations, and also provides that violation of any provision of the licensing law is a misdemeanor, and therefore punishable by criminal prosecution. (Of course, if the conduct complained of constitutes a serious crime under the criminal law statutes, there may be a felony involved.)

Under the rules and regulations promulgated by the real estate board, a violator is subject to disciplinary proceedings involving possible suspension or revocation of the license.

Some typical actions forbidden are:

1. Commingling (mixing) a client's funds with the broker's funds in one account.
2. Acting for both parties to a transaction without informing them both of that fact.
3. Advertising without showing that the advertiser is acting as a broker for another.
4. Performing legal services properly limited to an attorney-at-law.
5. Paying fees to one other than his salesman or another broker.

A typical state licensing law, that of North Carolina, is reproduced in Appendix C, together with the Rules and Regulations of that state's Real Estate Licensing Board.

11.

PROPERTY MANAGEMENT

A property manager is one who handles the operation of income-producing property for the owner. He does this for a specified fee, pursuant to a contract between him and the owner.

As a profession, property management is of relatively recent origin, but various factors have stimulated its growth to the point where today, there are not only many property management firms, but most real estate organizations engage in management as an integral part of their real estate activities.

The need for competent management was demonstrated forcibly in the Depression days of the early 1930's, when lending institutions were compelled to foreclose on vast numbers of properties. They found themselves burdened with properties they had neither the personnel nor the capability to handle.

Much realty is the subject of absentee ownership, another important reason for the growth of property management. Also, there has been a great increase in "syndicate" ownership, where individuals have pooled their resources to purchase substantial-size income-producing property. The individuals involved have neither the time nor the knowledgability needed to manage such properties.

The chief objective of the property manager is to obtain for the owner the highest net return from the property. This does not mean simply collecting rent; he must handle the overall maintenance of the property, so that over the life of the property, the net return is not adversely affected.

The typical management contract is a document setting forth in detail the rights and obligations of owner and manager. In addition to identifying the parties, describing the property, and specifying the term of the contract, the agreement spells out the extent of the manager's authority. Does he have the right to approve expenditures for maintenance and repairs? Must he obtain the owner's approval if an expenditure exceeds a certain figure? Does he have the authority to hire and fire maintenance personnel?

The manager's compensation is generally a percentage of the gross amount collected by him. A typical figure might be 5%.

The agreement will also provide for periodic reports—probably monthly—of receipts and disbursements.

(A typical management agreement is shown on the following page.)

The functions of the manager can be divided into three broad categories:

1. *Obtaining tenants.* In this connection, he must advertise, negotiate terms of leasing agreements, and maintain a satisfactory relationship with tenants during their tenancy.

2. *Maintaining the property.* This will probably include hiring necessary personnel. It will also include the physical care of the property. Additionally, the owner should be protected against risks which are insurable, and the manager will be responsible for obtaining such insurance as fire and extended coverage, general liability, workmen's compensation, and casualty.

3. *Maintaining financial records.* Periodic reports of rent collections, expenditures, etc. serve a dual purpose: they not only provide the owner with an accurate statement of income and expenditure, but they form the basis from which future planning may be accomplished. Often such figures will indicate trends which the owner can adjust to, or take advantage of, to maximize the return on his investment.

A property manager will usually prepare a budget for each property managed. The projections will be based either on the past experience with the particular property or with similar properties. Here the possibility for innovative thinking may give the manager the opportunity to point out to the owner ways by which his net return might be increased, perhaps through expenditures which will, in the long run, justify higher rentals. Such planning might be presented in the form of alternative budgets, in conjunction with the regular budget being presented.

Ideally, the budget should be an annual one, broken into monthly portions. This facilitates scheduling, particularly of such items as periodic maintenance and/or replacement of physical components. This also permits month-by-month as well as annual comparison with previous periods, for the purpose of determining where adjustments and revisions are called for.

PROPERTY MANAGEMENT AGREEMENT

THIS PROPERTY MANAGEMENT AGREEMENT, entered into this _____

day of _____ , 19 _____ , by _____

("Owner") and _____ ("Agent").
IN CONSIDERATION of the mutual covenants and promises each to the other made herein, the Owner does hereby employ the Agent exclusively, and the Agent does hereby accept the employment, to rent, lease, operate and manage the property more particularly described below and any other property the Owner may assign to Agent from time to time (the "Property") upon the following terms and conditions:
  1. **The Property**: Located in the City of _____ , County of _____ , State of North Carolina, being known and more particularly described as:

  Street Address: _____

  Apartment Complex: _____

  Other Description: (Room, portion of the above address, etc.) _____

  2. **Duration of Agency**: This Agreement and the Agency and employment hereby created shall commence and become effective on _____ , 19 _____ , and shall continue thereafter until terminated as provided herein.
  3. **Termination of Agency**: Either the Owner or the Agent may terminate the agency and employment created hereby by giving written notice of his intention to do so _____ days prior to the desired termination date. In the event the Owner terminates within _____ days of the commencement of this Agreement, he shall pay to the Agent a termination fee equal to one-half of one month's rent for each new tenant secured by the Agent on a weekly or monthly tenancy, plus, for any other lease agreements negotiated by the Agent, _____ percent (____ %) of the rents due from the unexpired term and _____ percent (_____%) of rents due from exercise of any options contained therein. No termination fee shall be required of the Owner for termination after the expiration of the number of days above specified and the Agent shall not be entitled to any percentage of any subsequently accruing rentals upon termination. Upon any termination of the Agreement by either the Owner or the Agent, each shall take such steps as are necessary to settle all accounts between them including the following: (1) the Agent shall promptly render to the Owner all rents then on hand after having deducted therefrom any Agent's fees then due and amounts sufficient to cover all other outstanding expenditures of the Agent incurred in connection with operating the Property; (2) the Agent shall render to the Owner records showing all tenants who paid security deposits under leases affecting the Property; (3) the Agent shall deliver to the Owner all tenant's leases and other instruments entered into on behalf of the Owner; (4) the Owner shall promptly pay to Agent any fees or amounts due the Agent under the Agreement and shall reimburse the Agent for any expenditures made and outstanding at the time of termination; and (5) the Owner shall notify all current tenants of the termination of the agency status.
  4. **Agent's Fee**: The Owner shall pay to the Agent each month during the existence of this Agreement the following percentages of gross rentals: _____ percent (____%) of gross monthly rentals on unfurnished apartments; _____ percent (____%) of gross monthly rentals on commercial and industrial property; _____ percent (____%) of all gross weekly rentals. The Owner also agrees to pay such additional monthly amounts to the Agent as may be necessary to provide that the Agent receives a minimum monthly charge of _____ Dollars ($_____) per tenant. The amounts due the Agent pursuant to this paragraph shall herein be referred to as the Agent's Fee and the Agent may deduct the Agent's Fee monthly from the gross rentals received before remitting the balance of the rentals to the Owner.
  5. **Agent's Authority**: The Owner hereby authorizes and empowers the Agent to perform such acts and take such steps as are necessary, in the Agent's opinion, to operate, manage, and lease the Property to the Owner's best advantage including, but not limited to:
  (a) Advertising the Property, displaying signs thereon, and renting the Property, including the authority to negotiate, execute, extend and renew leases in the Owner's name for terms not in excess of _____ year(s);
  (b) Instituting and prosecuting such judicial actions and proceedings as may be necessary to recover rents and other sums due the Owner from the tenants or to evict tenants and regain possession, including the authority, in the Agent's discretion, to settle, compromise and release any and all such judicial actions and proceedings;
  (c) collecting all rentals and other charges and amounts due or to become due under all leases covering the Property and giving receipts for the amounts so collected;
  (d) making or causing to be made any repairs which, in the Agent's opinion, may be necessary to preserve, maintain, and protect the Property; to maintain the facilities and services to the tenants as required by their tenancies; and to comply with any duties or obligations imposed upon the Owner by any local, state or federal law or regulation; including the authority to purchase such supplies and hire such labor as may be necessary in the Agent's opinion to accomplish such repairs;
  (e) performing any duties and exercising any rights conferred upon the Owner as Landlord under any leases entered into in connection with the Property; and
  (f) _____

  6. **Agent Covenants**: During the duration of this Agreement the Agent agrees:
  (a) To manage and operate the Property to the best of his ability devoting thereto such time and attention as may be necessary;
  (b) To furnish the services of his organization for renting, leasing, operating, and managing the Property;
  (c) To solicit and investigate all prospective tenants and to use his best efforts to secure and maintain tenants;

NORTH CAROLINA ASSOCIATION OF REALTORS, INC.

Standard Form No. 9
Revised 1978

(d) To offer the Property to the public for leasing in compliance with all state and federal housing laws, including but not limited to any federal and state laws and regulations prohibiting discrimination on the basis of race, color, religion, sex or national origin;

(e) To collect all monthly rentals and other charges due the Owner upon the Property and to make or cause to be made such repairs as he deems appropraite in order to preserve and maintain the Property and to comply with all lease requirements and obligations imposed upon the Owner by North Carolina law (N.C.G.S. § 42-42);

(f) To answer Tenant requests and complaints and to perform the duties imposed upon the Owner by law or pursuant to the tenant leases covering the Property.

(g) To render monthly statements of receipts, collections, expenses, charges and disbursements to the Owner and to remit to the Owner the balance of such receipts and collections; and

(h) _____

7. **Owner's Covenants**: During the duration of this Agreement the Owner Agrees:

(a) To advance to the Agent such sums as may be necessary to cover the costs of repairing the Property and maintaining it in a safe, fit and habitable condition as required by North Carolina law (N.C.G.S. § 42-42);

(b) To reimburse the Agent for any expenses actually incurred by him in operating, managing, and maintaining the Property, including but not limited to advertising expenses, general operating expenses, court costs, attorney's fees, and maintenance and supply expenses;

(c) Not to take any action or adopt any policy the effect of which would be to prevent the Agent from offering the Property for rental in compliance with all applicable federal and state laws and regulations, including but not limited to any federal and state laws and regulations prohibiting discrimination on the basis of race, color, religion, sex or national origin in the letting of the Property.

(d) To carry, at his expense, comprehensive general public liability insurance against any and all claims or demands whatever arising out of, or in any way connected with, the operation, leasing, and maintenance of the Property, which policies shall be written so as to protect the Agent in the same manner as the Owner and which shall be in the minimum

amounts of $ _____ for injury to or death of one person in each accident or occurrence, $ _____

for injuries to or death of more than one person in each accident or occurrence, and $ _____ for property damage in each accident or occurrence;

(e) To defend, indemnify, and save the Agent harmless from any and all damages, claims, suits, or costs whether for personal injury or otherwise, arising out of the Agent's management of the Property whether such claims are filed or damages incurred before or after the termination of this Agreement; and

(f) _____

8. **Security Deposits**: The Agent may in its discretion either (1) require tenants of the Property to make a security deposit in an amount as permitted by law to secure the tenants' obligations under leases of the Property (such security deposits shall hereinafter be referred to as "the Security Deposits".) or (2) forego the requirement that Security Deposits be made. If the

Agent requires such Security Deposits, they shall be placed in a trust account in the _____
                                                                                  (Owner's/Agent's)
name in a North Carolina bank or savings and loan association. The Agent shall be authorized to make withdrawals therefrom for the purpose of returning and accounting for them to the tenants and any interest earned by the Security Deposits while held

in such account shall belong to _____ . The Agent may, in his discretion and in lieu of depositing the
                                (Owner/Agent)
Security Deposits in a trust account, obtain, at the Owner's expense, a surety bond from a North Carolina insurance company securing the Agent's and Owner's obligation to account to the tenants for the Security Deposits in the manner provided by law. If such a surety bond is procured, the Agent may hold the Security Deposits in any manner which he deems appropriate. The Agent shall, during the duration of this Agreement, account to the tenants, in the manner as may be provided in the leases or by law, for any Security Deposits received by him. Upon the termination of this Agreement, the Agent shall either (1) turn over to the Owner all evidences of the trust account if the Security Deposits are placed in such an account or   (2) remit to the Owner a sum equal to all unrefunded Security Deposits received by the Agent if surety bonds are provided. Upon the occurrence of either event the Agent shall be relieved of any further liability with regard to the Security Deposits and the Owner shall assume the responsibility for thereafter accounting to the tenants for the Security Deposits.

9. **Existing Security Deposits**: Upon the commencement of this Agreement the Owner shall deliver to the Agent a list showing the current tenants of the Property who previously made Security Deposits under existing leases of the Property and the amounts they deposited. Simultaneously therewith, the Owner shall either: (1) place the Security Deposits held under

existing leases in a trust account in the _____ name and authorize the Agent to make withdrawals
                                          (Owner's/Agent's)
therefrom for the purpose of returning them to the current tenants as required by their leases or by law; or (2) supply the Agent with evidence of a surety bond from a North Carolina insurance company securing the Owner's obligation to return the Security Deposits to the proper tenants as required by law. In the event the Owner elects to furnish a surety bond pursuant to this paragraph, he shall thereafter advance to the Agent such sums as may be necessary from time to time to allow the Agent to return the deposits to the existing tenants as required by their leases or by law.

10. **Notices**: Any notices required or permitted to be given hereunder shall be written and shall be mailed by certified mail by each party to the following addresses:

Owner: _____

Agent: _____

11. **Form**: The Owner and Agent hereby acknowledge that their Agreement is evidenced by this form contract which may contain some minor inaccuracies when applied to the particular circumstances of the parties. The Owner and Agent agree that the courts shall liberally and broadly interpret this Agreement, ignoring minor inconsistencies and inaccuracies, and that the courts shall apply the Agreement to determine all disputes between the parties in the manner which most effectuates their intent as expressed herein. The following rules of construction shall be applied: (1) handwritten and typed additions or alterations shall control over the preprinted language when there is an inconsistency between them; (2) the Agreement shall not be strictly construed against either the Owner or the Agent; (3) paragraph headings shall be used only for convenience of reference and shall not be considered as a substantive part of this Agreement; (4) words in the singular shall include the plural and the masculine shall include the feminine and neuter genders, as appropriate; (5) no waiver of any breach of any obligation or promise contained herein shall be regarded as a waiver of any future breach of the same or any other obligation or promise; and (6) the invalidity of one or more provisions of this Agreement shall not affect the validity of any other provisions hereof and this Agreement shall be construed and enforced as if such invalid provisions were not included.

IN WITNESS WHEREOF the parties hereto have set their hands and seals the day and year first above written.

AGENT:

_____ (SEAL)

OWNER:

_____ (SEAL)

12.

THE REAL ESTATE OFFICE

There are about half a million licensed real estate brokers in the United States, and an even greater number of licensed salesmen. Although many may not be actively engaged in the industry, those figures give us some idea of the recent unusual growth of the field.

In addition to rather severe licensing requirements, some states have gone even further in the protection of the public, and have enacted statutes providing for the establishment of "recovery funds" from which customers, defrauded by a broker, may be compensated. Even in states without such funds, brokers generally must post a bond in order to engage in brokerage activities, so that even in situations where a broker has had his license revoked for improper practices, and is without resources, an aggrieved customer will not go uncompensated.

Operating a real estate brokerage firm may be accomplished through the sole proprietorship, the partnership, or the corporation. Each has advantages and disadvantages. The sole proprietorship enjoys the benefit of flexibility and ease of control, simply because the owner is one individual who can arrange and rearrange as he sees fit. At the same time, that owner is individually liable for the obligations of his firm, and his personal limitations of capability and finances limit his firm accordingly.

The partnership form has the obvious advantage of pooling the resources of the individual partners, both as to finances and capability. Aside from the disadvantage, however, of possible personal disagreements, the chief drawback of the partnership is the fact that each partner is personally liable for obligations of the firm; his personal assets can be reached by creditors of the firm.

The corporate form of ownership provides pretection against personal liability. No member of the firm is personally liable for obligations of the corporation; the most that a co-owner of the firm can lose is the amount of his investment. There is, however, an additional tax burden in that corporate earnings are really taxed twice—once when the corporation pays income tax on its profits, and again, when stockholders pay tax on the dividends paid to them out of those profits. In addition, there are costs in organizing the corporation.

Aside from office personnel, it is the sales associate who forms the backbone of the real estate office. Whether full-time or part-time workers, licensed salespersons handle the various day-to-day activities that determine the financial success of the organization.

Most salespersons are "independent contractors" rather than "employees." This means that they are free to arrange their working activities as they see fit, are compensated strictly on a commission basis, and pay their own expenses such as automobile, telephone, etc. Independent contractors cannot participate in company pension or profit-sharing plans, nor is the employing broker responsible for income tax or social security deductions from the salesperson's compensation.

The test generally applied to determine whether a salesperson is an independent contractor or an employee is one of control; the employing broker determines the goals, but does he have the right to control the means by which the salesperson achieves the goal? If he does, then an employer-employee relationship exists, even though the intention of the parties might have been to create an independent contractor status.

Most salespersons are compensated strictly on a commission basis. This usually consists of a pre-arranged split of the commission between the salesperson and the employing broker. Although the range may vary widely, the most common arrangement is a 50-50 split. If the firm is a member of a multiple listing service, the fee to the service would first be deducted from the commission before the split is computed.

It is also common practice for the salesperson who obtained the listing to receive a small share of the commission, perhaps 10%. Local custom, and the particular provisions of the multiple listing membership agreement, would determine the apportionment of commission, but an example might be the following:

Selling price of property	$50,000
Commission rate	6%
Multiple listing service (MLS) fee	$20

In this case, the commission to be divided would be $3,000 (6% of $50,000) less $20 payable to MLS. This leaves $2,980 to be divided.

If listing broker A was also the selling broker, and his salesman B procured the sale, then A and B would divide $2,980 on a 50-50 basis (assuming this was the ratio called for in the employing agreement).

Suppose A is the listing broker, but another broker C is the selling broker. Depending on the local arrangement, the division of the commission might be something like the following:

Total commission:	$3,000
Fee to MLS	20
Net commission to be divided	$2,980
Listing salesman (10%)	$ 298
Listing broker A (30%)	$ 894
Selling broker C (60%)	$1,788

The selling broker C (assuming his firm has a 50-50 arrangement with its salespeople) would share the $1,788 equally with the selling salesperson.

The salesperson works under a written agreement with the employing broker. This is important not only to set forth the terms of the arrangement, but also to make clear, where the status is that of independent contractor, that such is the case. This is valuable to the salesperson who, on his or her personal income tax return, would certainly wish to take items such as car expenses as deductions.

Offices with more than one salesperson must have some means of fairly allocating unsolicited prospects among the sales personnel. When a potential customer telephones or walks in off the street, he must be referred to a salesperson. Some offices use a rotating system in which each salesperson takes a turn in handling such inquiries. The obvious disadvantage here is that a salesperson who is out of the office misses opportunities; since the objective of any progressive office is to have the salespersonnel out showing property or obtaining listings (and not just sitting behind a desk) there is a conflict between the need to be out of the office, and the desire to be at one's desk to take advantage of his "turn at bat."

Another method, perhaps more popular, is to assign each salesperson a "duty day" in the office. That person remains in the office that day and all "walk-ins" are referred to him; if that person is required to leave the office on important company business, any other salesperson may handle the prospect on behalf of the absent person. The "duty days" are planned for the entire month, and equitably distributed among the personnel. In a well-run office, with a good relationship among the salespersons, this system virtually eliminates any feelings of inequity or favoritism, and aids in promoting morale.

Greater and greater attention is being paid to the aptitude of potential salespersons. The typical brokerage firm—even those smaller firms with a sales force of perhaps three or four—are requiring applicants to take tests which indicate the likelihood of success, based upon a "personality profile" of factors which would affect real estate work, either favorably or unfavorably.

There is, of course, a cost to the firm for each "selling desk" it maintains. Aside from that desk's proportionate share of general office overhead, there are the particular costs associated with that salesperson. The firm cannot expect much from a new member of the sales staff for a period of perhaps six months. Beyond that point, however, a salesperson will be expected to "pull his weight."

An interesting concept has developed recently, and has gained strong favor, particularly in California. Under this plan, rather than sharing commissions with the salesperson, the firm furnishes space and all the office essentials, but computes a selling desk's proportionate share of office costs, adds in a reasonable profit for the firm, and allocates this total cost to the desk as a debit against which it credits the salesperson with the *total* amount of commissions on his sales. In other words, the salesperson receives the total commission, but must be sufficiently productive to offset the company's costs and its reasonable profit.

Generally in the larger organizations there are no "house accounts"— clients whose business is credited to the firm, rather than to a salesperson. The principals (owners) of the brokerage firm will often lend their assistance to salespersons, but with no intention of depriving the salesperson of the commission. Even in smaller firms, the trend is away from principals keeping clients for "the firm;" the promotion of incentive and high morale among the sales personnel is, in the long run, beneficial for the firm.

In the very large firms, of course, there often is little contact, if any, between top management and the individuals on the sales force; usually sales managers are directly responsible for the work of salespersons under them, much as in industrial activity.

An interesting development utilized by some offices is the "farm" system, whereby a salesperson develops a particular neighborhood (perhaps a residential development) to canvass for listings. That person maintains continuous personal contact with that area, and he or she will be thought of whenever anything involving real estate arises there. Some typical activities by the salesperson might include sending a letter of welcome to new arrivals; writing letters of personal introduction to all residents, followed by a brief personal call; maintaining complete records of all sales in the area (including those made by owners or other brokers). If a listing is obtained (and the client consents) letters might be sent to the client's neighbors suggesting that they advise friends of the availability of the property. Upon the arrival of a new homeowner, the salesperson (with the consent of the homeowner) might send out to other owners in the development a letter introducing the newcomers and giving some superficial information about them.

All of these activities serve to identify the salesperson as a "specialist" in the particular area, and keep his or her name constantly in the minds of the property owners.

The typical brokerage office will conduct periodic meetings of the sales staff—probably weekly—to go over the status of listings, and to encourage discussion of matters affecting the individual staff members and the office generally. Additional incentives and morale-boosters such as contests for sales performance, with awards such as paid vacation trips, are common. As in any organization depending on sales performance, the primary objective of the firm is to develop a sales force that can maintain a cooperative spirit while being individually competitive and productive.

13.

SELLING REAL ESTATE

For those who are considering a career in real estate sales, a word of caution is in order. Among the general populace there exists the common misconception that real estate offers an easy, pleasant and exciting way to overnight riches. It is surprising to find how many think of a real estate broker's typical day as a few hours spent either in a luxurious office or driving around and meeting interesting people, interspersed with collecting and depositing fat commission checks.

It certainly is possible for a successful broker or salesperson to have earnings well above the general "average." The key, however, lies in that word *successful,* and that in turn depends on several factors, not the least of which is knowledge.

As we mentioned in an earlier chapter, most states are moving toward stricter requirements for licensing of brokers and salesmen. *Product knowledge* is the key, and whether acquired through education, experience or a combination thereof, it is a prerequisite to a successful career in the field.

But let us assume that you have the requisite general knowledge of real estate. *Product knowledge* does not end there. It is essential that you know all there is to know about a particular parcel for which you are attempting to find a buyer. The old saying goes, "a house well listed is half sold;" which is simply another way of saying that when your information is total you have the means with which to handle every aspect of your potential deal successfully.

The most desirable property, in the eyes of prospect A, may turn prospect B completely off. Differences in taste and need are apparent to anyone. The successful salesperson, bearing this in mind, attempts to educate himself as to buyer motivation. What makes people buy what they do? Why do potential buyers frequently respond emotionally to a product, rather than rationally? The salesperson, fortified with some understanding of the motivating forces behind human behavior, is better equipped to focus on the particular attributes of a property that he feels will elicit a positive response in his prospect. For example, *pride of ownership* may be a motivational force of wide general appeal; but regardless of how well a residential property satisfies this need, if situated on a heavy-traffic street, its appeal may not be as great to a couple with three small children. Such a buyer's motivating force—concern for children's safety—may best be satisfied by a home, though perhaps more modest, on a quiet, dead-end street.

Salespersons are coming to understand more and more that their ultimate success depends not on *selling* but upon *helping the prospect to buy*, primarily because working in that direction creates in the prospect a feeling of trust and confidence, which is half of the sale itself. How, then, can you help that prospect to buy? Only by understanding what he is motivated to buy, and why he is so motivated.

No text or article on salesmanship ever omits the subject of handling and overcoming objections. In selling real estate, the potential range of objections raised by prospects is even greater than might be encountered in other fields; when you consider the number of features and attributes of any particular parcel, it is easy to see why. A good lawyer really prepares his opponent's case, as well as his own. When you have answers ready to counter the prospect's objections, the impact of the objection is materially lessened, if not eliminated altogether.

Certain basic objections are encountered again and again, regardless of the particular property in question—such as confusion about the advisability of owning versus renting. The successful salesperson always has at his fingertips the facts and figures—updated to conform to current economic developments—to counter this objection. As to objections relating to the specific property under scrutiny, our previous advice regarding total knowledge of the property is again applicable. Only by being thoroughly conversant with every detail surrounding the subject property can the salesperson be fortified with the means by which a prospect's objections can be handled and disposed of smoothly and efficiently.

There are many attributes that might explain the difference between the productive salesperson and the would-be producer. The following summarizes two basic factors:

1. The ability to obtain listings by following a pre-planned system of prospect accumulation, bolstered by an understanding of the motivations and objectives of the seller.
2. Producing an acceptable buyer through the ability to understand buyer motivations and to relate these to the subject property by thorough knowledge of the property.

GLOSSARY OF WORDS AND PHRASES COMMONLY USED

ABSTRACT OF TITLE
A synopsis of the history of title to a property, including references to all documents creating or affecting rights in the property.

ACCELERATION CLAUSE
A clause in a document which provides for a balance due to become immediately payable upon a certain condition.

ACKNOWLEDGMENT
A written statement before a notary public or similar officer, by which one acknowledges that an instrument executed was his free and voluntary act.

ACRE
A measure of land equalling 43,560 square feet.

ADMINISTRATOR
A person appointed by the court to settle the estate of one who died intestate (without a will) (feminine form: administratrix).

AD VALOREM
"According to value." Property taxes constitute an ad valorem tax, since they are based on the value of the property.

ADVERSE POSSESSION
The continuous, open and notorious possession of land, hostile to the record owner, which can ripen into ownership if maintained for the statutory period of time required.

AFFIDAVIT
A written statement sworn to before a notary public or other similarly-empowered person.

AFFIRMATION
A declaration, similar to an oath, made by one whose religious beliefs forbid the taking of an oath.

AGE OF MAJORITY
See LEGAL AGE

AGENCY	A relationship in which one person (the agent) is authorized to act on behalf of another (the principal).
AGENCY COUPLED WITH AN INTEREST	An agency in which the agent has an interest in the property involved.
AGENT	One authorized to act on behalf of another.
AGREEMENT OF SALE	The contract of sale between buyer and seller, setting forth the terms and conditions of the sale.
AIR RIGHTS	The right to use or control the air space over the particular property.
AMENITIES	The qualities or attributes of property, other than material benefits. (Location, satisfaction in the pleasure derived from beauty of design, etc.)
AMORTIZATION	The liquidation of a sum by periodic installment payments.
APPRAISAL	An estimate of value; the process by which a measure of value is obtained.
APPRAISAL BY CAPITALIZATION	Same as INCOME APPROACH
APPRAISAL BY COMPARISON	Same as MARKET DATA APPROACH
APPRAISAL BY SUMMATION	Same as COST APPROACH
APPRECIATION	Increase in value.
APPURTENANCE	That which is part of something else; an appurtenance to land would be included in a transfer of the land.
ASSESSED VALUATION	The value assigned to property by the appropriate official for the purpose of determining the tax on it.
ASSESSMENT	A charge against real property.
ASSIGNEE	One to whom a contract is assigned.
ASSIGNMENT	The transfer to another of a right or contract.
ASSIGNOR	One who transfers by assignment.

ASSUMPTION FEE	A charge made by the mortgagee when an existing mortgage loan is being assumed by a new buyer of property.
ASSUMPTION OF MORTGAGE	The act of a buyer of property by which he expressly undertakes the payment of the obligation secured by the mortgage on the property.
ATTORNEY AT LAW	One licensed to practice law who is authorized to represent another in legal proceedings.
ATTORNEY IN FACT	One who is authorized to act for another having been given this authority by a document called a power of attorney.
AVULSION	The sudden removal of soil from one property to another by the action of water.
BALLOON PAYMENT	A large final payment on some contractual obligation.
BENCH MARK	A permanent marker, fixed in the ground, placed by surveyors.
BENEFICIARY	One designated to receive the benefits of some contractual arrangement.
BEQUEST	A gift, by will, of personal property.
BILL OF SALE	A document by which title to personal property is transferred.
BI-MONTHLY	Every two months.
BINDER	An agreement involving a down payment on the purchase of property, contemplating a later execution of a formal contract or deed.
BLANKET MORTGAGE	A mortgage covering more than one parcel of property.
BLIGHTED AREA	An area where property values are being severely affected by economic influences such as depreciating structures, the influx of residents of lower economic levels, and similar factors.
BLIND ADVERTISEMENT	An advertisement in which the advertiser is not identified.

BLOCKBUSTING	An activity, prohibited by law, by which attempts are made to persuade owners of property to sell, by implying that racial or ethnic changes in the neighborhood will drastically lower the value of their property.
BONA FIDE	Made in good faith; having a firm basis, without fraud.
BOND	An obligation under seal. In real estate, the security would be a mortgage (or deed of trust) affecting the property.
BREACH	The failure to perform a duty or contractual obligation.
BROKER	A person or firm who, for a fee, negotiates the sale, exchange, or lease of real property for another.
BUILDING CODE	Governmental regulations (city, county, or state) setting forth standards of building and construction which must be followed.
BUILDING LINE	A line fixed at a certain distance from the street line in front (or from the side line of the lot) beyond which a structure may not project.
CAPITAL	Wealth; funds invested in a business enterprise.
CAPITAL ASSETS	Assets used in an income-producing activity.
CAPITAL GAIN	Profit realized on the sale of property (other than goods sold in the course of business).
CAPITALIZATION	A process by which a future periodic income is converted into a present value (as in the "income approach" to appraisal and valuation).
CAPITALIZATION RATE	The rate of interest used in determining value based upon the income approach.
CAPITAL LOSS	Loss realized on the sale of property (the opposite of capital gain).
CASH FLOW	The remaining disposable income from an investment, after allowing for all expenses, taxes and debt payments.
CAVEAT EMPTOR	"Let the buyer beware." The principle that the buyer buys at his own risk.

CERTIFICATE OF ELIGIBILITY	A certificate attesting to the fact that one is eligible for a V.A. (Veteran's Administration) mortgage loan.
CERTIFICATE OF NO DEFENSE	(Also called "estoppel certificate"). Document executed by a mortgage debtor acknowledging the amount of debt and its validity.
CERTIFICATE OF OCCUPANCY	A document issued by an appropriate city or county agency certifying that a building conforms to the local code of structural requirements, and that it is therefore approved for occupancy.
CERTIFICATE OF REASONABLE VALUE	A document furnished by the Veteran's Administration appraising property in connection with an application for a V.A. mortgage loan.
CERTIFICATE OF REDUCTION	A document executed by a mortgagee attesting to the present remaining balance of the mortgage; usually furnished by the seller to the buyer of the property.
CERTIFICATE OF TITLE	A document furnished by an attorney at law as to the state of title to property, based upon a search of the records.
CESTUI QUE TRUST	The one for whose benefit property is being held by a trustee; the beneficiary of the trust.
CHAIN	A unit of measure equalling 66 feet.
CHAIN OF TITLE	The history of a particular parcel of land, based upon the recorded documents affecting it.
CHATTEL	An item of personal property.
CHATTEL MORTGAGE	A mortgage affecting personal property.
CHATTEL REAL	A contractual right such as a leasehold which relates to real property, but is personal property.
CLEAR TITLE	See MARKETABLE TITLE
CLOSED-END MORTGAGE	A mortgage which does not provide for a further loan after the original loan has been reduced (the opposite of an *open-end mortgage*).
CLOSED MORTGAGE	A mortgage which does not give the borrower the privilege of paying off the entire loan before maturity.

CLOSING

The consummation of the transaction; usually refers to the procedure by which title to property is transferred.

CLOSING COSTS

Expenses involved in the process of closing title.

CLOSING STATEMENT

A summary of the financial details of the title closing, accounting for all funds received and expended. Copies are furnished to the buyer and seller.

CLOUD ON TITLE

Some defect or encumbrance on the title to property representing a possible claim which would affect the owner's title.

COLOR OF TITLE

Some written document purporting to indicate title in one who is claiming title, but which is defective. Also referred to as *apparent title*.

COMMINGLING OF FUNDS

The situation in which a broker's own funds, as well as those of his clients, are on deposit in the same account. Generally prohibited by state licensing laws.

COMMISSION

The fee earned by a broker for his services, usually a percentage of the selling price (or rent amount, in the case of a lease).

COMMITMENT

A binding pledge or promise.

COMMON LAW

The body of law in England, based upon general custom and usage, that developed through court decisions, and was brought here and followed by the colonists. Except as modified by statutes, the common law prevails in all but a few states.

COMMON WALL

See PARTY WALL

COMMUNITY PROPERTY

A principle, followed in a few states, by which spouses share equally in property acquired by each during the period of their marriage. Certain types of acquisitions are excepted.

COMPETENT PARTIES

Persons who have legal capacity to enter into binding agreements.

COMPOUND INTEREST

Interest paid not only on the principal sum, but also on the interest that has accumulated.

CONCURRENT OWNERSHIP	The situation where two or more persons own the same property at the same time. (See JOINT TENANCY, TENANCY IN COMMON, TENANCY BY THE ENTIRETY, COMMUNITY PROPERTY.)
CONDEMNATION	The proceeding by which property is taken by governmental authority for some public use. (Also, a determination by some authorized agency that a structure is unfit for use.)
CONDITIONAL COMMITMENT	In FHA (Federal Housing Administration) mortgage loans, the promise of the agency to make a definite loan amount to a future borrower conditioned on that borrower's satisfactory credit standing.
CONDOMINIUM	An arrangement whereby one owns in fee simple a unit of a multi-unit structure (an apartment in a multiple dwelling structure), and is a tenant in common, along with other owners, of the areas used by all.
CONFORMITY, PRINCIPLE OF	In appraisal, the theory that a property's maximum value is achieved if the character of its use is similar to that of other properties in the area.
CONSIDERATION	Something of value that forms the basis for a contractual obligation. It is a required element in any valid, enforceable contract.
CONSTRUCTION LOAN	A loan made for the purpose of having a structure built. The funds usually are made available in installments as various stages in the construction process are reached.
CONSTRUCTIVE EVICTION	Any breach of a lease agreement by the landlord that renders the property unfit for tenant's use.
CONSTRUCTIVE NOTICE	Notice of a particular fact given by putting the fact on public record, either by filing or recording in the appropriate office or by publication in a newspaper.
CONTINGENT	Dependent upon some fact or event.
CONTRACT	An agreement between two or more persons, legally enforceable.
CONTRACT FOR DEED	See LAND CONTRACT

CONTRACT RENT	Rent set forth in a lease.
CONVENTIONAL LOAN	A mortgage loan not involving a government agency.
CONVEY	To transfer title to property.
COOPERATIVE	A term used to describe the arrangement whereby one, by purchasing shares of stock in a corporation which owns a multi-unit dwelling structure, obtains the right to occupy a unit in that structure.
CORRELATION	In appraisal, the weighting of the three approaches to valuation for the purpose of arriving at the final estimate of value.
COST APPROACH	One of the three methods of property appraisal, by which the replacement cost of the property is obtained, depreciation subtracted, and land value then added. (Also called summation approach.)
COUNTER OFFER	A response to an offer which incorporates some modification of that offer.
COVENANT	A promise or guarantee whereby the promisor agrees to do, or to refrain from doing, some act.
COVENANT OF QUIET ENJOYMENT	The guarantee of a grantor, in a warranty deed, that the grantee's possession and use of the property will not be disturbed by any claims of others.
C.P.M.	Certified Property Manager. A designation granted by the Institute of Property Management to qualified persons.
CREDITOR	One to whom a debt is owed.
CUL-DE-SAC	A street or alley closed at one end (also dead-end).
CURABLE DEPRECIATION	Property loss in value which can be rectified through repair or remodeling.
CURTESY	The husband's common-law right in property of his wife upon her death. Superseded by statute in many states.
DAMAGES	The award of a court to one whose rights have been violated by another.
DEBTOR	One who owes a debt.
DECEDENT	One who has died.

DECLARATORY JUDGMENT	A judgment or decree of a court officially declaring the validity and legal effectiveness of a particular situation.
DECREE	An official pronouncement of a court of equity.
DEDICATION	The process by which an owner of land grants title to it for some public use, and this is accepted for such use by the proper government officials.
DEED	An instrument which transfers title to real property when properly signed, sealed, and delivered.
DEED OF TRUST	A deed held by a trustee as part of a mortgage loan arrangement, used in some states in place of the common mortgage form. The trustee holds title for the benefit of the lender, subject to the defeat of the title by the repayment of the loan.
DEFAULT	The failure to perform an obligation.
DEFAULT JUDGMENT	See JUDGMENT BY DEFAULT.
DEFENDANT	A party against whom legal action is brought.
DEFERRED MAINTENANCE	In appraisal, the need for repair or rehabilitation of a structure which has not been attended to.
DEFERRED PAYMENTS	Payments to be made at a future time.
DEFICIENCY JUDGMENT	A judgment for the balance of a debt where the sale of the property used as security was insufficient to satisfy the debt.
DELINQUENT	Past due.
DEMISE	The transfer of an estate by a lease.
DEPOSIT	Earnest money. A portion of the purchase price given to show good faith on the part of the buyer.
DEPRECIATION	The loss of value in property caused by age, physical wear and tear, or economic and/or functional obsolescence.
DEPRECIATION RATE	The percentage of a base amount to be applied annually.
DETERIORATION	The physical worsening of a structure, normally caused by use and weather.

DEVELOPER — One who improves real property, usually by building upon it. He may or may not have been the original "subdivider." (q.v.)

DEVELOPMENT — A subdivision.

DEVISE — A gift of real property by will.

DEVISEE — One to whom land is devised by will.

DISCOUNT — To sell an instrument of debt (such as a promissory note) for less than the face amount.

DISPOSSESS — Proceeding to remove one from land by legal action.

DISTRAINT — The seizure of personal property as security for an unpaid obligation such as rent.

DOCUMENTARY STAMP — A revenue stamp issued for payment of a tax on documents.

DOMICILE — One's legal residence; the place which one considers his permanent abode (also Legal Residence).

DOMINANT TENEMENT — The property held by one benefitting from an easement (also called *dominant estate*).

DONEE — One to whom a gift is made.

DONOR — One who makes a gift.

DOWER — The common-law right a wife has in property of her husband at his death; superseded by statute in many states.

DOWN PAYMENT — The deposit customarily given by a purchaser of real estate at the time the contract of sale is signed.

DUPLEX — A residential stucture designed for occupancy by two families; in some areas referred to as a "two family house."

DUPLEX APARTMENT — An apartment dwelling on two levels.

DURESS — Unlawful force, or threat of force, which compels one to sign an agreement, or perform any act, against his will.

EARNEST MONEY — A deposit or down payment given by a purchaser.

EASEMENT	A right to use the land of another for a particular purpose, such as a right-of-way across the land.
EASEMENT IN GROSS	An easement in the nature of a temporary license or permission which does not "run with land."
ECONOMIC LIFE	The period of time over which improved property is reasonably expected to yield a return.
ECONOMIC OBSOLESCENCE	The loss in property value caused by factors outside the property itself, such as zoning regulations, changes in neighborhood character, and economic conditions.
ECONOMIC RENT	The amount of rent a particular property would bring if it were vacant and available, based on rents generally prevailing in comparable properties.
EFFECTIVE AGE	In appraisal, the age of a structure as measured by its physical condition rather than by its actual chronological age.
EFFECTIVE DATE	The exact date upon which something takes place or takes effect.
EFFECTIVE GROSS INCOME	The gross income from property less an allowance for vacancies and uncollectable rents.
EJECTMENT	A form of legal action by the owner of real property to regain possession from one unlawfully on the property.
EMBLEMENTS	Crops produced by the land.
EMINENT DOMAIN	The right of government to take private property for public use upon payment of fair compensation.
EMPLOYMENT CONTRACT	The listing of property with a broker by which the property owner employs the services of the broker to sell or rent the property. (See LISTING AGREEMENT.)
ENCROACHMENT	The intrusion of a structure, or a part thereof, on the land of another.
ENCUMBRANCE	Anything affecting or limiting the title or use of property, such as mortgages, liens, easements.
ENDORSEMENT	See INDORSEMENT

EQUITABLE TITLE	The concept of the purchaser's interest in property after execution of the contract of sale but before the closing of title. Although not yet the holder of legal title, the purchaser, since he has the contractual right to title, may be subject to certain benefits or risks accruing during this period.
EQUITY	The financial value represented by property, less any liens against it; also, in law, legal doctrines of rights and principles of fairness applicable beyond the strict confines of statutory and common law.
EQUITY OF REDEMPTION	The right of a mortgagor who has defaulted to regain his property even after his delinquency. The time period varies among the states.
EROSION	The wearing away of land through actions of the elements.
ESCALATOR LEASE	A lease providing for an increase or decrease in rent based upon certain contingencies (See also INDEX LEASE).
ESCHEAT	The process whereby property of a deceased who left no will and no heirs reverts to the state.
ESCROW	The procedure by which something is deposited with one not a party to the transaction, to be delivered upon the satisfaction or performance of some condition.
ESCROW ACCOUNT	An account in which funds being held in escrow are deposited.
ESCROW FOR TAXES AND INSURANCE	In situations where the mortgagee handles payment of taxes and insurance, a portion of the monthly mortgage payments sufficient to pay these items as they come due.
ESTATE	The degree of one's interest in real property; also, a term used to represent the total assets left by a deceased.
ESTATE AT SUFFERANCE	See TENANCY AT SUFFERANCE
ESTATE AT WILL	See TENANCY AT WILL
ESTATE FOR LIFE	See LIFE ESTATE

ESTATE FOR YEARS   See TENANCY FOR YEARS

ESTATE IN FEE   See FEE SIMPLE

ESTATE OF FREEHOLD   See FREEHOLD ESTATE

ESTATE TAX   A tax imposed on an estate for the transferring of property to heirs of the deceased.

ESTOPPEL   A legal principle by which a particular claim or defense asserted by someone is held ineffective because of some prior contradictory position taken by him.

ESTOPPEL CERTIFICATE   See CERTIFICATE OF NO DEFENSE

ET AL   "And others."

ET UX   "And wife."

EVICTION   The procedure by which one in possession of land is ousted. (See also CONSTRUCTIVE EVICTION.)

EXCLUSIVE AGENCY   Same as exclusive listing contract. Giving one broker the sole right to sell property on behalf of the owner, with the owner reserving the right to sell the property himself without being obligated to pay commission.

EXCLUSIVE RIGHT TO SELL   Giving a broker the sole right to sell the property, so that he earns commission even if the property is sold by the owner himself.

EXECUTOR   One named in a will to carry out the provisions of the will. (Feminine form: executrix)

EXISTING MORTGAGE   A mortgage that has not been discharged, and is therefore in existence against a particular property.

EXPRESS   To state by spoken or written words. The opposite of "implied."

EXPRESS EASEMENT   An easement specifically set forth in an instrument.

EXTENDED COVERAGE   In title insurance, a form of coverage broader than that in the basic type of policy.

EXTENSION AGREEMENT	An agreement by which the term of an existing mortgage is extended.
FEDERAL HOME LOAN BANK	A federal agency established to act as a central source of credit for savings institutions.
FEDERAL HOME LOAN MORTGAGE CORP.	Known as "Freddie Mac." Federal agency established to operate in the secondary mortgage market by buying and selling existing mortgages.
FEDERAL HOUSING ADMINISTRATION (F.H.A.)	A federal agency through which high loan-to-value ratio loans may be approved, with the agency insuring the loan for the lender at a small annual premium to the borrower.
FEDERAL LAND BANK	A federal agency system which makes long-term loans on farm land.
FEDERAL NATIONAL MORTGAGE ASSOCIATION	Commonly known as "Fanny Mae." A privately owned corporation, under federal regulation, which buys and sells mortgages in the secondary market.
FEDERAL RESERVE SYSTEM	A federal agency which serves banks belonging to the system primarily by acting as a clearing house for checks and as a source of credit. It can influence the general availability of funds through its rate of interest charged for loans to member banks.
FEDERAL SAVINGS & LOAN INSURANCE CORPORATION	(F.S.L.I.C.) A federal agency which insures accounts in federally chartered savings and loan associations and in those state-chartered associations which have qualified. Accounts are insured up to $40,000 each.
FEE	(Same as FEE SIMPLE or FEE SIMPLE ABSOLUTE) The highest degree of land ownership. There is no time limitation on the title, and it is freely transferable by sale or by will.
FIDUCIARY	One who, because he occupies a position of trust, is held to the highest degree of loyalty and good faith. A real estate broker is a fiduciary with regard to his principal.
FIRM CONTRACT	A valid, binding agreement.
FIRM PRICE	A price determined by the seller, and which is not subject to negotiation.

FIRST MORTGAGE
Also called SENIOR MORTGAGE. A mortgage which takes precedence over any other mortgage claims.

FIXED RENT LEASE
Also called FLAT LEASE OR STRAIGHT LEASE. A lease which provides for a fixed rent amount during the term of the lease.

FIXED CHARGES
In property ownership, those expenses such as real property taxes and insurance which are not subject to month-to-month fluctuation.

FIXTURE
Something attached to the land or a structure in a permanent manner so as to make it part of the real estate.

FLAT LEASE
See FIXED RENT LEASE

F.N.M.A.
See FEDERAL NATIONAL MORTGAGE AS-SOCIATION

FORECLOSURE
A legal proceeding whereby property mortgaged as security for a loan is sold to satisfy the unpaid debt.

FOREIGN CORPORATION
A corporation which received its charter in a state other than the one in which it is operating.

FORFEITURE CLAUSE
In a contract, a clause providing for the loss of something upon failure to perform an obligation. In a lease, generally the right of the landlord to declare the tenant's right of possession forfeited upon non-payment of rent.

FRAUD
In law, the intentional misstating of a material fact to induce action on the part of another which results in some loss or damage.

FREE AND CLEAR
A phrase used to denote a situation in which property is owned in fee and not subject to any encumbrances.

FREEHOLD
The estate of ownership of real property either in fee simple or a life estate; distinguished from a leasehold, or non-freehold estate.

FRONTAGE
The length of footage of real property along a street or road.

FRONT ELEVATION — In architectural design, the drawing showing the front of a structure.

FRONT FOOT — In valuation, a measure of value represented by one foot of frontage and extending back to the depth of the lot.

FRONT FOOT VALUE — The price of a lot expressed per front foot.

FUNCTIONAL OBSOLESCENCE — The lessening of value of a structure caused by its outmoded design, absence of desired amenities, and similar factors.

GENERAL LIEN — A right given to an unpaid creditor to proceed against any property owned by the debtor. A judgment is the most common example. (Compare with SPECIFIC LIEN.)

GENERAL WARRANTY DEED — A deed in which the grantor promises to protect the grantee against anyone claiming an interest in the property.

G.I. LOAN — A mortgage loan, guaranteed by the Veterans Administration, available only to veterans of the armed forces. (Same as V.A. LOAN or V.A. MORTGAGE.)

G.I. MORTGAGE — See G.I. LOAN

GINNIE MAE — A phrase used to describe G.N.M.A. (See GOVERNMENT NATIONAL MORTGAGE ASSOCIATION.)

GOOD TITLE — See MARKETABLE TITLE

GOVERNMENT NATIONAL MORTGAGE ASSOCIATION — A government corporation, under the Department of Housing and Urban Development, which assists low cost federally assisted residential housing through special mortgage loan programs. It also acts to attract funds for mortgage loans by backing securities issued against blocks of FHA and VA loans.

GOVERNMENT SURVEY — (Also called RECTANGULAR SURVEY) A system of land measurement and identification applicable in most states other than the New England and Atlantic Coast states. Survey lines known as meridians and base lines form the basis for further subdivision into townships, which are further subdivided into sections. Each section contains one square mile (640 acres).

GRACE PERIOD — An additional time period within which to satisfy some obligation, beyond the date normally called for.

GRADUATED LEASE — A lease, usually long-term, providing for periodic increases or decreases in the rent.

GRANT — A transfer of real property.

GRANTEE — One to whom real property is transferred.

GRANTOR — One who transfers real property.

GROSS INCOME — The total income from property, before deduction of expenses.

GROSS INCOME MULTIPLIER — See GROSS RENT MULTIPLIER

GROSS LEASE — A lease by which the lessee pays rent and the lessor is responsible for all expenses relating to the property (taxes, insurance, mortgage payments, etc.).

GROSS RENT MULTIPLIER — A figure used in obtaining an appraised value of real property. It is the number obtained by dividing the selling price of comparable property by its monthly rent.

GROUND LEASE — A lease agreement for unimproved property, often providing for the erection of a building by the lessee.

GROUND RENT — The rent paid for, or earnings attributable to, the land itself, exclusive of any structure.

GUARANTEED LOAN — A loan, the payment of which is guaranteed by a third party, in the event of a default by the borrower. A V.A. loan is an example (compare INSURED LOAN).

HABENDUM CLAUSE — That portion of a deed, sometimes called the "to have and to hold clause" which sets forth the extent of the estate being conveyed.

HEIR — One who inherits, either by will or under a statute.

HEIRS AND ASSIGNS — Phrase used in a deed conveying a fee simple estate, showing that the grantee will own "forever", having the right to transfer ownership by will or otherwise.

HEREDITAMENTS — All inheritable interests in property, both corporeal (land itself) and incorporeal (a right, such as an easement).

HIGHEST AND BEST USE — That use of land most likely to produce the greatest net return over a period of time.

HOLDOVER TENANT — A tenant who, after expiration of his lease, remains in possession of the premises.

HOLOGRAPHIC WILL — A will in the handwriting of the testator.

HOMEOWNERS POLICY — An insurance policy designed specifically for homeowners; there are five basic forms with varying types and degrees of coverage.

HOMESTEAD RIGHT — Real property used as a home and entitled to certain limited protection against claims of creditors, depending upon particular state statutes.

HOMESTEAD EXEMPTION — A reduction of real property tax against property used as the homestead, granted in some states.

HOUSING CODE — Local laws setting certain standards for dwelling structures.

H.U.D. — Department of Housing and Urban Development; a federal agency which seeks to aid local communities, chiefly by the use of loans and grants to help solve such problems as slum areas, pollution of residential areas, etc.

IMPLIED CONTRACT — A valid and enforceable agreement implied from the conduct of the parties, rather than from the written or oral expression of the agreement.

IMPLIED WARRANTY — A promise or guarantee imposed by law, although not specifically stated in the contract.

IMPOUND ACCOUNT — (Also called ESCROW ACCOUNT) An amount included as a portion of the monthly payment made by the mortgagor to the mortgagee, which will provide the mortgagee with the funds with which to pay the taxes and insurance as they come due. These funds are considered escrow or trust funds.

IMPROVED LAND	Land upon which some improvement (structures, walls, fences, etc.) has been placed.
INCHOATE INTEREST	An anticipated interest; one that is not yet legally effective.
INCOME	The return, usually monetary, that is produced by the use of some capital good.
INCOME APPROACH	A method of property valuation by which the net income produced by the property is converted into a valuation figure by use of a capitalization rate.
INCOME PROPERTY	Property, whether residential or commercial, that is owned for the purpose of monetary return to the owner.
INCURABLE DEPRECIATION	A loss in value of a structure caused either internally or externally, which is incapable of being cured, or which would cost more to cure than the resulting increase in value.
INCURABLE TITLE	A defect in title, rendering the title unmarketable, which cannot be cured.
INDEMNIFY	To make good, or compensate for, some loss of another.
INDENTURE	A written agreement between parties.
INDEPENDENT CONTRACTOR	One who is engaged by another to perform certain acts, but whose work and time are not subject to constant control; he is, therefore, not an employee.
INDEX LEASE	A lease in which the rent stipulated is subject to increase or decrease in conformity with the movement of a particular economic index such as The Consumer Price Index.
INDICATED VALUE	Property value as indicated by one or more of the approaches to valuation.
INDORSEMENT	A signature placed on the back of a negotiable instrument (promissory note or draft) for the purpose of transferring ownership of the instrument to another.
INDUSTRIAL PARK	An area specifically laid out, zoned, and used for industry.

INFANT

A minor. One under the legal age of majority which traditionally was 21, but which has been lowered in most states to 18.

INHERITANCE TAX

A tax against property passing by inheritance. It is generally imposed by states against those inheriting and would constitute a lien against the property (thus preventing the transfer of marketable title) until paid. (Compare with ESTATE TAX.)

INITIATION CHARGE

See ORIGINATION CHARGE

INJUNCTION

A court order restraining one from performing a particular act.

IN LIEU OF

In place of.

IN PERSONAM

Against a person. A judgment, for example, against a person rather than a right assertable against a thing (such as a parcel of real estate).

IN REM

Against a thing. A lien (against a specific property) upon which a judgment is obtained ordering the sale of the property, would create a judgment in rem.

INSIDE LOT

A lot not located on a corner.

INSOLVENT

Unable to pay all one's debts.

INSTALLMENT LAND
CONTRACT

A contract calling for payment by the buyer in periodic installments, at the completion of which title will be conveyed to him by the seller.

INSTALLMENT NOTE

A promissory note calling for payment in periodic installments over a specified period of time.

INSTITUTIONAL
LENDER

An institution, such as a bank, which makes real estate loans.

INSTRUMENT

A written document having legal effect.

INSURABLE TITLE

A title capable of being insured by a title insurance company.

INTEREST

The price paid for the use of money.

INTERSTATE LAND
SALES FULL
DISCLOSURE ACT

Federal legislation enacted in 1968 to protect buyers of lots in states distant from their homes. It regulates the interstate sale of lots by requiring registration of information concerning the property.

INTESTATE — Without a will.

INVALID — Void, having no legal effect.

INVESTMENT PROPERTY — Real property owned for the purpose of profiting from the income returned by the property.

JOINT AND SEVERAL OBLIGATION — Where two or more persons are obligated as a group and also each individually, so that the party to whom they are obligated may elect to sue any one or all of them.

JOINT TENANCY — Co-ownership of the same property by two or more persons, with the right of survivorship (q.v.). (See also TENANCY IN COMMON and TENANCY BY THE ENTIRETY.)

JOINT VENTURE — An association of two or more persons for a specific business project or transaction.

JUDGMENT — The final decision of a court in a legal proceeding.

JUDGMENT BY DEFAULT — A court decision in favor of a party because of the failure of the other party to appear and answer the complaint.

JUDGMENT CREDITOR — One in whose favor a court has awarded a monetary sum.

JUDGMENT DEBTOR — One against whom a court has made a monetary award.

JUDGMENT DOCKET — The formal court records of judgments awarded. To "docket" a judgment means the formal entry of the judgment into the records, thereby creating a lien against property of the judgment debtor.

JUDGMENT LIEN — The right of a judgment creditor to proceed against property of the judgment debtor in order to satisfy the judgment.

JUDGMENT PROOF — A phrase used to describe the condition of one against whom a judgment will be ineffective because of his lack of assets.

JUDICIAL SALE OF PROPERTY — (Also COURT-ORDERED SALE) The sale of property by order of a court.

JUNIOR — Something that is lesser in standing, or subordinate to some other, such as a junior mortgage (second mortgage), the claim of which must await the satisfaction of the senior (first) mortgage.

JURISDICTION — The authority to handle a given matter. A court has jurisdiction over those matters properly within its legal scope of control.

JUST COMPENSATION — A phrase used in the taking of private property under the right of eminent domain, by which is meant the compensation paid to the property owner for the taking.

LACHES — A legal term describing one's failure, or unreasonable delay, in asserting a legal claim or right. It is the basis for such laws as a Statute of Limitations (q.v.).

LAND — The physical surface of the earth, together with anything permanently affixed to it or in it.

LAND CONTRACT — (Also called CONTRACT FOR DEED) An agreement for the sale of land, calling for the buyer to make periodic installment payments to the seller, at the completion of which the buyer will receive a deed.

LANDLOCKED — A phrase describing the condition in which a parcel of land is surrounded by land of others, and has no means of ingress or egress of its own.

LANDLORD — The owner of leased property; the LESSOR.

LANDMARK — An object used as a boundary mark in surveying or describing real property.

LAND USE CONTROL — The planned control by government, through zoning and similar restrictions, of the use to which land is put. The purpose is to provide for orderly development that will provide optimal benefit to the community.

LAPSE — The termination of some claim or right because of some failure of action.

LATE PAYMENT CHARGE — An additional charge imposed for failure to make an installment payment on time, as in mortgage payments.

LATERAL SUPPORT	The support which the soil of a landowner gives to the land of the adjoining landowner.
LEASE	A contract by which possession and use of land is granted by the owner to another.
LEASE ASSIGNMENT	A contract by which a lessee transfers to another his entire interest as lessee for the remaining term of his lease.
LEASEHOLD	The legal interest of a lessee.
LEASE TERMINATION	The ending of a lease either by the expiration of the term specified, or by agreement of the parties, or by a breach of a condition followed by the aggrieved party's rescission.
LEGACY	Personal property bequeathed by a will.
LEGAL ACTION	A court proceeding instituted by an aggrieved party against another.
LEGAL AGE	The age at which a minor reaches majority and achieves legal capacity in the eyes of the law. Traditionally 21, but now 18 in most states.
LEGAL DESCRIPTION	A descriptive statement of measurement, location, or distances sufficient to identify a particular parcel of land.
LEGAL OWNER	One whose ownership is a matter of record.
LEGAL RESIDENCE	See DOMICILE
LEGATEE	One who inherits personal property under a will.
LESSEE	One who rents property under a lease agreement; the tenant.
LESSOR	See LANDLORD
LESS-THAN-FREEHOLD	See NON-FREEHOLD
LET	To lease or rent.
LEVY	To assess against, as in taxes; also, to proceed against a debtor's property in satisfacation of the debt.
LIABLE	Accountable or responsible.
LICENSE	Personal permission granted to enter another's land, usually temporary and revocable.

LIEN — The right of a creditor to proceed against property of the debtor in satisfaction of the debt.

LIENOR — One who holds a lien.

LIFE ESTATE — An estate in land representing ownership for the duration of a named person's life.

LIFE TENANT — One who holds a life estate.

LINK — A unit of land measurement equal to 7.92 inches.

LIQUID ASSETS — Assets readily convertible into cash.

LIQUIDATE — To convert into cash by sale.

LIQUIDITY — The ability to convert assets into cash.

LIQUIDATED DAMAGES — An amount agreed upon in a contract, to be paid by one who breaches the contract.

LIS PENDENS — A document, recorded in the appropriate county office, giving notice of a pending legal action affecting real property.

LISTING — (Also LISTING CONTRACT or LISTING AGREEMENT) A contract between a principal and a broker by which the services of the broker are engaged. Most often the principal is a property owner who wishes the broker to find a buyer for the property.

LITIGATION — The process of a lawsuit.

LOAN AGREEMENT — A document setting forth the terms and conditions of the loan.

LOAN APPLICATION — The documents containing the information submitted by an applicant for a loan, upon which the lender's decision will be based.

LOAN CLOSING — The consummation of the loan agreement by the lender making the funds available to the borrower, and recording the mortgage document.

LOAN COMMITMENT — The written document by which a lender agrees to make a loan. The specific amount, rate of interest, and any other terms and conditions will be included.

LOAN CORRESPONDENT — One who represents a non-resident lender in handling loans.

LOAN FEE

A charge made by the lender for making the loan (also called ORIGINATION CHARGE).

LOAN-TO-VALUE RATIO

The ratio that a loan amount bears to the appraised value of the mortgaged property.

LOCUS SIGILLI

"Place of the seal." In documents "under seal," the place at which the seal of the signer would be placed. In present day documents, this is usually indicated by the letters "L.S." immediately after the line for the signature.

LONG-TERM CAPITAL GAIN

For purposes of federal income tax computation, gain on the sale of capital assets held for more than one year. Such gains receive preferential tax treatment.

LONG-TERM LEASE

A lease term of long duration, generally more than ten years.

LOT LINE

The boundary line of a lot.

L.S.

See LOCUS SIGILLI

M.A.I.

Member, American Institute of Appraisers. One who, by satisfying certain qualification requirements, is given this designation.

MAKER

One who executes a promissory note.

MALL

A public walk; also, the common area surrounding the individual business establishments comprising a shopping center, sometimes enclosed.

MANAGEMENT AGREEMENT

A contract between a property owner and an agent calling for the agent to manage the property.

MARGINAL LAND

Land whose income return barely covers the cost involved in its use.

MARKETABLE TITLE

(Also called MERCHANTABLE TITLE or GOOD TITLE) That title, sufficiently free of liens or encumbrances, that a purchaser would be legally bound to accept.

MARKET DATA APPROACH

(Also called MARKET APPROACH or COMPARISON APPROACH). A method of appraisal by comparing the subject property with similar properties which have recently been sold.

MARKET VALUE — The highest price a property would command on the open market, with neither buyer nor seller acting under any unusual pressure of circumstances.

MASTER PLAN — A comprehensive statement covering the future development of a community in conformity with desired physical and social objectives.

MATERIAL FACT — In contractual agreements, any fact, relating to the subject of the agreement, that would affect a party's decision to engage in the transaction.

MATERIALMAN'S LIEN — See MECHANIC'S LIEN

MECHANIC'S LIEN — A right given by statute to one who has furnished labor or materials for improvement of a particular property; he has the right, if unpaid, to proceed against the property for the satisfaction of his claim. (Also known as LABORER'S and MATERIALMAN'S LIEN)

MERCHANTABLE TITLE — See MARKETABLE TITLE

MERIDIANS — In the Rectangular or Government Survey system, the north-south lines from which locational measurements are calculated.

METER — In the metric system, a unit of measurement equalling 39.37 inches.

METES AND BOUNDS — A method of property description by use of distance measurement, direction, and boundaries.

MILE — A measure of distance equalling 5280 feet.

MILL — One-tenth of one cent. Property tax rates may be stated in terms of mills per dollar of assessed valuation.

MINERAL RIGHTS — The right to take minerals from land; the right may be held by one other than the landowner.

MINIMUM LOT ZONING — A zoning regulation stating the minimum lot size upon which a structure may be erected.

MINOR — A person not of full legal age; in most states, one under 18.

MISREPRESENTATION — A false or misleading statement.

MODERNIZATION	The replacement, in a structure, of outmoded or worn equipment or parts of the structure.
MONTH-TO-MONTH TENANCY	A lease for a month, renewable each month (if both parties are agreeable) for an indefinite number of such monthly terms.
MONUMENT	A fixed object, either natural or artificial, used by surveyors as a point from which to calculate distance and direction.
MORATORIUM	A temporary suspension, usually in connection with the performance of an obligation, so that a debtor, for example, would be relieved of his obligation to pay during the period of the moratorium.
"MORE OR LESS"	In a property description, where this phrase is used following a statement of the number of acres, it is intended to provide for a possible small deviation from the actual number.
MORTGAGE	To make property security for the repayment of a loan; also, the document itself by which this security transaction is accomplished. In some states, the document used in place of a mortgage is the Deed of Trust (q.v.).
MORTGAGE COMMITMENT	The formal declaration by a lending institution that it will make a mortgage loan on particular property on the terms and conditions specified.
MORTGAGE COMPANY	A company dealing in existing mortgages.
MORTGAGE CORRESPONDENT	One who acts as an agent or representative of an institution which makes mortgage loans.
MORTGAGEE	The lender in a mortgage loan transaction.
MORTGAGE INSURANCE	Insurance protecting a mortgagee against financial loss resulting from non-repayment of the loan.
MORTGAGEE'S TITLE INSURANCE	Insurance protecting a mortgagee against financial loss resulting from a defect in title.
MORTGAGE REDUCTION CERTIFICATE	See CERTIFICATE OF REDUCTION
MORTGAGOR	A borrower who uses property as security for the debt.

MULTIPLE LISTING AGREEMENT
A listing agreement whereby other brokers (members of a group to which the listing broker belongs) are permitted to sell the listed property.

MULTIPLE LISTING GROUP
A membership group of real estate brokers in a particular area. Listings obtained by a member are circulated so that all other members may act on them, with any resulting commission to be divided between the listing broker and the selling broker.

N.A.R.
National Association of Realtors (Formerly NAREB, National Association of Real Estate Boards).

NEGOTIABLE INSTRUMENT
A draft or promissory note having certain characteristics which make it readily transferable in commercial activity.

NET INCOME
The return yielded by income-producing property, after deduction of expenses.

NET LEASE
A lease in which the tenant is obligated to pay all expenses of the property, such as taxes, insurance, and maintenance, in addition to rent.

NET LISTING
A listing agreement calling for a certain amount to be received by the seller, and anything above that amount to be retained by the broker as commission. This is generally frowned upon, and in a few states is prohibited by law.

NET NET LEASE
A lease in which the tenant is obligated to pay, in addition to rent, all charges and expenses of the property, including mortgage payments of principal and interest.

NON-CONFORMING USE
A use of property not permitted by the zoning law, but which existed before the enactment of such law, and is therefore generally permitted to continue.

NON-FREEHOLD ESTATE
(LESS-THAN-FREEHOLD ESTATE) A leasehold or right to possession and use of property for a limited time. Unlike the fee simple estate, the holder is not the owner of the property.

NOTARIZE
To take an acknowledgment or attestation in connection with a legal document, in one's capacity as a Notary Public.

NOTARY PUBLIC   One authorized by law to take acknowledgments of legal documents and to administer oaths.

NOTE   See PROMISSORY NOTE

NOTICE TO QUIT   Notice given to a tenant to vacate the property.

NOVATION   A new contract that substitutes for an old one. Usually where an original party to a contract is replaced by a new party, and all three agree to the substitution. This is distinguished from a simple assignment of a contract, where the assigning party might retain some liability.

NUISANCE   A legal term denoting activity whose continuance is offensive to others or impairs their rights. May be either public or private in nature.

OBLIGEE   One in whose favor an obligation exists.

OBLIGOR   One who is obligated to another.

OBSOLESCENCE   Loss in value caused by a reduction in desirability, either internal (see FUNCTIONAL OBSOLESCENCE) or external (see ECONOMIC OBSOLESCENCE).

O.L.T. POLICY   Owners, landlords and tenants liability insurance policy.

OPEN-END MORTGAGE   A mortgage that allows the borrower, after a portion of the loan has been repaid, to re-borrow up to the amount of the original loan.

OPEN HOUSING   The phrase describing the situation in which dwellings are available to all, without unfair discrimination as to color, etc.

OPEN LISTING   A listing agreement by which the seller is free to engage the services of other brokers, or to sell the property himself.

OPEN MORTGAGE   A mortgage which permits the borrower to pay off the loan before maturity without any penalty. (See PREPAYMENT PENALTY.)

OPERATING EXPENSES   All expenses incident to the ownership of income-producing property, except mortgage loan payments.

OPTION	An agreement whereby, for some consideration, one is given the right to buy or lease property within a specified time.
OPTIONEE	One to whom an option is given.
OPTIONOR	One who gives an option.
ORAL	Verbal, not in writing.
ORDINANCE	A local law, such as one enacted by a municipality.
ORIGINATION FEE	See LOAN FEE
OUTBUILDINGS	Structures other than the main one, but within the boundaries of the specific property.
OVERHANG	That part of a roof extending beyond the wall of the structure.
OVER-IMPROVEMENT	An improvement whose cost is not justified by a commensurate increase in the return produced (compare with UNDER-IMPROVEMENT).
OVERT	Open to view; public.
OWNER-MANAGEMENT CONTRACT	See MANAGEMENT AGREEMENT
OWNER'S EQUITY	The value of the owner's interest in property, over and above any liens against it.
OWNER'S TITLE POLICY	A policy issued to the owner, insuring his title for the value of the land and improvements, effective for as long as his ownership continues.
PACKAGE MORTGAGE	A mortgage that includes personal property (such as equipment) in addition to the real property.
PARAMOUNT TITLE	Title that is superior to any other.
PARCEL	A particular piece of real property, separable from any other by reason of its description.
PAROL	Verbal, not written, such as "parol evidence."
PAROL EVIDENCE RULE	A rule of law which generally prohibits the use of oral testimony to alter the terms of a written agreement. Exceptions are sometimes made to permit unclear or ambiguous language to be explained.
PARTIAL RELEASE	The release of a part of mortgaged property from the effect of the mortgage, so that it is no longer

subject to the lien. Common where a subdivider, with a blanket mortgage on the sub-division, sells an individual lot, and obtains the release of that lot by the payment to the mortgagee of a pre-arranged sum.

PARTIALLY AMORTIZED MORTGAGE
A mortgage that provides for amortizing a part of the loan, followed by a lump sum payment of the balance.

PARTICIPATION AGREEMENT
The agreement by which two or more lenders share in a single mortgage loan.

PARTITION ACTION
A legal proceeding which seeks to have property sold, and the proceeds divided among the co-owners.

PARTNERSHIP
An association of two or more persons for the purpose of carrying on a business for profit.

PARTY WALL
A wall built on the line dividing two adjoining properties, to be used by both owners. (Also called COMMON WALL.)

PASS-THROUGH SECURITIES
Securities issued, backed by a pool of government-insured or guaranteed mortgages, so called because payments of principal and interest on the mortgages are "passed through" to the holders of the certificates in proportion to their holdings.

PATENT
The original grant of land to an individual by a sovereign government. So called because title was granted by "letters patent."

PAYEE
One to whom a monetary obligation, such as a promissory note, is payable.

PAYOR
One who pays a monetary sum that is due.

PER ANNUM
Annually, or per year.

PER CAPITA
Literally, "per head," meaning for each person.

PERCENT
An amount defined in terms of its proportion to one hundred.

PERCENTAGE
An amount expressed as a rate per hundred.

PERCENTAGE LEASE
A lease in which the amount of rent is determined by the volume of business done by the lessee.

PERCOLATION TEST
A test used to determine the water-absorbing capability of soil.

PERIMETER	The outer boundary of a surface.
PERIODIC TENANCY	A leasehold providing for an indefinite number of definite terms, such as a month-to-month or year-to-year tenancy. It is terminable by either party upon proper notice.
PERJURY	Making a false statement under oath.
PERSONAL PROPERTY	Things of a movable nature, not real property. Also called CHATTELS or PERSONALTY.
PETITION	A formal request to a court, governing body, or official agency.
PHYSICAL DEPRECIATION	Loss of value in property, caused by wear and tear, and action of the elements.
P.I.T.I.	Principal, interest, taxes, and insurance. Commonly used to designate those items included in typical monthly mortgage payments.
PLAINTIFF	The party who brings a lawsuit against another.
PLANNING BOARD	An agency whose function is to determine and plan for the future development of a community, and to make regulatory recommendations to that end. (Sometimes called PLANNING COMMISSION.)
PLAT	A map of a sub-division usually filed in the appropriate county office, showing the exact lots into which the tract was divided.
POINTS	A fee charged by a lender in connection with a V.A. or F.H.A. mortgage loan to compensate for the lower interest rate usually required in those types of loans. One point is equal to 1% of the loan amount.
POLE	A measure of length equal to 16.5 feet.
POLICE POWER	The inherent right of the state to regulate the use of private property in the interest of the general welfare of the public.
POST-DATE	To date a document with a date later than the one on which it is executed.
POWER OF ATTORNEY	A document by which one grants to another the power to act in his place.

POWER OF SALE CLAUSE	In a deed of trust, the clause giving the trustee the right to sell the property in the event of the borrower's default.
"PRE-FAB" HOUSE	A prefabricated house, manufactured and partially assembled, then delivered to the homesite.
PRE-CUT HOUSE	A house whose structural components are manufactured and delivered to the homesite, and must then be assembled and completed.
PREPAYMENT CLAUSE	A clause in a mortgage, giving the borrower the right to pay the mortgage debt before it is due.
PREPAYMENT PENALTY	An additional charge assessed by the mortgagee if the borrower repays the mortgage loan before the due date.
PRESCRIPTIVE RIGHT	A right acquired by the passage of a prescribed period of time.
PRIMARY MORTGAGE MARKET	The market for loans made by lenders to borrowers.
PRINCIPAL	One who employs an agent; in loans, the amount of the loan as distinguished from the interest thereon.
PRINCIPAL MERIDIAN	In the rectangular system of land description, one of the designated main survey lines running North and South.
PRIVATE MORTGAGE INSURANCE	Insurance offered by private insurance companies insuring mortgages. Distinguished from government-insured mortgages such as in F.H.A. loans.
PROBATE	(From the Latin "proved") The court procedure by which a will is proved valid, and the estate of the deceased administered.
PROCURING CAUSE	That factor chiefly responsible for the successful consummation of the property transaction. The broker who is the procuring cause would presumably be entitled to the commission.
PROMISSORY NOTE	A writing by which one promises to pay a definite sum of money at a certain future time.
PROPERTY BRIEF	In appraisal, a detailed written description of property, including structural and financial data.

PROPERTY LINE   A boundary line of property.

PROPERTY TAX   A tax levied against property, based upon the value of the property ("ad valorem," q.v.).

PRO RATA   In proportion.

PRORATION   The apportioning of obligations such as taxes, insurance, etc. at the title closing, so that buyer and seller each pay their respective shares based upon their respective periods of ownership of the property.

PROXY   A designation by which one is authorized to act, usually to vote, on behalf of another; also, the person so designated.

PUBLIC DOMAIN   Real property owned by government.

PUBLIC UTILITY   See UTILITY EASEMENT
  EASEMENT

PUNITIVE DAMAGES   In a lawsuit, damages awarded by the court in excess of the amount needed to compensate the aggrieved party; it is ordered by way of punishment, and is applicable in few instances.

PURCHASE MONEY   A mortgage "taken back" by the seller as part of
  MORTGAGE   the purchase price of the property. In effect, the seller becomes a lender to the purchaser.

QUARTERLY   Four times a year, or once every three months.

QUASH   In law, to annul or make ineffective, usually applied to a court order of that effect.

QUIET ENJOYMENT   The right of an owner of property to the possession and use of his property without interference or adverse claims.

QUIET TITLE SUIT   A court proceeding brought to determine the ownership of real property. The final determination will effectively remove any clouds from the title.

QUITCLAIM DEED   A deed by which the grantor conveys his interest, if any, to the grantee, with no warranties whatsoever.

QUORUM   The number of members of a constituted group, association, etc. who must be present at a meeting for business to be validly transacted. Usually set by the group's rules, by-laws, etc.

QUO WARRANTO
A legal proceeding brought, usually by the state, to require the surrender or forfeiture of some official designation of office, or a charter (such as a corporation's charter).

REAL ESTATE
Real property; land and improvements to the land, including things permanently affixed to it, either man-made or natural.

REAL PROPERTY
A term generally used synonymously with Real Estate.

REALTOR®
A registered trademark denoting a licensed real estate broker who is a member of a local board affiliated with the National Association of Realtors.

RECORDING
The entering of a document in a public record.

RECTANGULAR SURVEY
See GOVERNMENT SURVEY

RECOVERY FUND
A fund established in some states from which compensation is paid to persons suffering losses caused by licensed brokers.

REDEMPTION
The process by which a property owner who has lost his property by reason of foreclosure may get back his title by payment of arrears plus interest and penalties.

REFINANCING
The obtaining of a new loan, or the extension of an existing one.

REFORMATION
A legal proceeding to correct an error in some legal document.

REGISTER OF DEEDS
A county office in which instruments affecting real property are recorded.

REHABILITATION
Restoring a structure to good condition, with no change in basic style and plan.

RELEASE
To give up some right or claim.

RELEASE CLAUSE
See PARTIAL RELEASE CLAUSE

REM	See IN REM
REMAINDERMAN	One who is to receive title to property at the termination of a present life estate.
REMAINING ECONOMIC LIFE	In appraisal, the number of remaining years a structure is expected to be economically useful.
REMODEL	To change the plan or form of a structure.
RENOVATE	To restore to its former condition.
RENT	The consideration paid for the possession and use of real property.
REPLACEMENT COST	The cost to replace a structure with one having the same utility, but with materials and design conforming to current standards.
REPRODUCTION COST	The present cost of reproducing an existing structure exactly, with the same materials and design.
RESCIND	To annul or cancel.
RESCISSION	The act of annulling or cancelling; a party to a contract generally may rescind the contract upon breach by the other party.
RESERVATION OF RIGHTS	A process by which a grantor of real property may retain certain rights in himself.
RESTRICTION	A limitation, either in a deed or separate instrument, affecting the use of the property.
RESTRICTIVE COVENANT	The clause in a deed or separate instrument constituting a limitation on the use of the property.
RETROACTIVE	Effective as of a prior date or time.
REVENUE STAMP	In many states, a stamp required to be purchased and affixed to deeds, thus constituting a tax on transfers of real property.
REVERSION	A right to future ownership or possession retained by one who grants to another; he is said to have a *reversionary interest*.
REZONING	Changing the zoning classification of a property or area, thus affecting the type of use permitted.
RIDER	An amendment or addition to a document.

RIGHT OF SURVIVORSHIP	The right of a joint owner of property by which he acquires the interest of a deceased co-owner.
RIGHT OF WAY	The right to cross another's land for purpose of access, maintenance of utilities, etc.
RIPARIAN RIGHTS	The rights of an owner of property bordering water to the use of the water, its bed and banks.
RISK RATE	In the income approach to appraisal, a constituent part of the overall capitalization rate, designed to compensate the investor for the risk of loss of his investment.
ROD	A measure of length equal to 16.5 feet (same as POLE).
RULE OF THUMB	A rough guide or rule based upon experience.
RURAL	Pertaining to the country, rather than to an urban area.
SALE AND LEASEBACK	A transaction in which the owner of property, usually a business operation, sells the property and simultaneously leases it from the buyer on a long-term basis.
SALES CONTRACT	The contract of sale between buyer and seller setting forth the terms of the sale.
SATISFACTION	The discharge of some legal obligation, such as repayment of a mortgage loan.
SATISFACTION PIECE	A document acknowledging the discharge of a mortgage.
SEAL	An impression made on a document attesting to its execution. In modern usage, the word ''seal'' or the letters ''L.S.'' after a signature constitute the equivalent of the impression.
S.E.C.	See SECURITIES AND EXCHANGE COMMISSION
SECONDARY MORTGAGE MARKET	The activity of buying and selling existing mortgages.
SECOND DEED OF TRUST	A Deed of Trust that is subordinate or second to a prior Deed of Trust.

SECOND MORTGAGE — A mortgage that is second, or subordinate, to a prior mortgage called a "first" mortgage.

SECTION — In the rectangular or government survey system of land description, a tract of 1 square mile, or 640 acres.

SECURED OBLIGATION — An obligation for which security such as property is present.

SECURED PARTY — The lender whose loan is secured.

SECURITIES — Instruments evidencing rights of ownership (such as stock certificates) or debt (bonds).

SECURITIES AND EXCHANGE COMMISSION — A federal agency which regulates dealings in securities.

SECURITY — Property posted to guarantee the performance of some obligation.

SECURITY INTEREST — That interest which a creditor has in the property of the debtor.

SEISIN — The possession of land under a claim of ownership.

SEMI-ANNUAL — Twice a year; every 6 months.

SEMI-MONTHLY — Twice a month.

SENIOR MORTGAGE — A first mortgage.

SEPTIC TANK — An underground tank for draining off sewage from a home, where a local sanitary sewer system is not available.

SERVIENT TENEMENT — (Also called SERVIENT ESTATE) The land in which an easement is held by another landowner.

SETBACK — The distance from a street or curb line to a point on property; a setback ordinance prohibits erection of a structure within that area.

SEVERALTY OWNERSHIP — Ownership by one person.

SHERIFF'S DEED — (Sometimes MARSHAL'S DEED) A deed given to a purchaser of real property at a court-ordered sale of real property to satisfy a debt.

SHORT-TERM CAPITAL GAIN	Profit realized from the sale of property held for less than one year.
SHORT-TERM LEASE	Generally, a lease of less than ten years duration.
SIGNATORY	One who signs a document.
SIMPLE INTEREST	Interest computed only on the amount of the original principal.
SINKING FUND	A fund of money, usually acquired by setting aside periodically a proportion of income, which will ultimately extinguish a debt or pay for some improvement.
SITE	A particular location for some planned use or purpose.
SPECIAL ASSESSMENT	A charge levied by a public authority against real property to pay the cost of some public improvement by which the property benefits.
SPECIAL WARRANTY DEED	A deed in which the grantor guarantees the title against any claims or defects arising during his ownership of the property.
SPECIFIC LIEN	A lien that attaches only to a specific parcel of property (compare with GENERAL LIEN).
SPECIFIC PERFORMANCE	An action for specific performance is a remedy for a breach of obligation, seeking not money damages, but a court order requiring the defendant to perform whatever he is contractually obligated to do.
SPOT ZONING	Zoning by which specific property is zoned differently from the area surrounding it.
SQUATTER	One who occupies the land of another without his consent.
STANDARD METROPOLITAN AREA	A county or group of counties containing at least one city of 50,000 population or more.
STATUTE	A law passed by a legislative body.
STATUTE OF FRAUDS	A statute, existing in all states, which lists certain types of contracts that must be in writing to be enforceable.

STATUTE OF LIMITATIONS	A statute prescribing a time period during which legal proceedings may be commenced; after the expiration of such period, no action may be instituted.
STRAIGHT LEASE	See FIXED RENT LEASE
STRAIGHT-LINE DEPRECIATION	A method of depreciation by which a constant percentage of the total amount is applied each year. Under this method an item with a 20-year useful life would depreciate 5% per year.
SUB-CONTRACTOR	One to whom a contractor contracts out part or all of his existing contract.
SUB-DIVIDER	One who divides a tract into smaller parcels for the purpose of sale.
SUBDIVISION	A tract of land that has been divided into small parcels for use as residences or businesses (also called a DEVELOPMENT).
SUBJECT TO MORTGAGE	A condition in a purchase of property by which the purchaser acquires the property with knowledge that the mortgage remains a lien against the property, but he does not assume personal liability on the mortgage note. In the event of foreclosure, the most he can lose is the property. (Compare ASSUMPTION OF MORTGAGE.)
SUBJECT TO DEED OF TRUST	See SUBJECT TO MORTGAGE
SUBLEASE	The leasing of premises by a lessee to a third party for a portion of the lessee's lease term.
SUBLESSEE	See SUBTENANT
SUBLETTING	The act of entering into a sublease.
SUBORDINATE	To subordinate is to make something secondary to something else.
SUBORDINATION	The act of making something subordinate.
SUBORDINATION CLAUSE	A clause, typically in mortgages or leases, providing that a party's rights are secondary or subordinate to some other subsequent right. For example, a subordination clause in a lease might render the tenant's rights subordinate to a later-created mortgage on the property.

SUBPOENA	An order directing a person to appear in a judicial proceeding.
SUBROGATION	The doctrine by which one acquires the legal rights of another, as where an insurer, by paying the insured for his loss may "step into the shoes" of the insured for the purpose of proceeding against the one who caused the loss.
SUBSTITUTION	In appraisal, the principle that no normal buyer will pay more for a property than the cost of obtaining a substitutable property of equal desirability that is available.
SUBTENANT	One who leases property from a tenant; the tenant in a sublease.
SUBURBAN	Relating to the area on the outskirts of, or adjacent to, an urban or city area.
SUFFERANCE	See TENANCY AT SUFFERANCE
SUMMATION APPROACH	See COST APPROACH
SUM-OF-THE-YEARS DIGITS	A method of computing depreciation. It is a declining balance method that produces the larger proportion of depreciation during the earlier years of ownership of property. For each year, it is computed by multiplying the cost figure by a fraction, the numerator of which consists of the remaining years of the property's economic life, and the denominator of which is the sum of the digits representing the years of the total economic life.
SUMMONS	A legal notice of complaint directed to someone, and served on him (usually personally, although in some cases permitted to be mailed or published) requiring an answer within a prescribed time. Failure to answer generally results in a judgment for the complaining party (plaintiff) by default.
SUNDAY LAWS	Laws enacted prohibiting business activity on Sundays. Also referred to as BLUE LAWS.
SUPPLEMENTARY PROCEEDINGS	A proceeding by which a judgment debtor (one against whom a money judgment has been obtained) may be questioned under oath in order to determine whether he has any assets which might be seized by the creditor to satisfy the judgment.

SURETY — One who guarantees another's performance of some obligation.

SURETY BOND — The contract by which a surety guarantees to indemnify an insured for loss occasioned by another's failure to perform.

SURRENDER — A term used in cancellation of a lease, whereby the premises are surrendered to, and accepted by, the landlord, either by abandonment by the tenant or mutual agreement of the parties.

SURVEY — The determination of the boundaries of a property through measurement.

SURVIVORSHIP — See RIGHT OF SURVIVORSHIP

SYNDICATE — A combination of individuals who undertake a particular venture which otherwise would be too large for each individually. Similar to JOINT VENTURE.

TANGIBLE PERSONAL PROPERTY — Items of personal property which have physical substance.

TAX — Any compulsory payment levied by government to support its activity.

TAX BASE — The total assessed valuation of all property within a specific district or government area.

TAX DEED — The deed given to the buyer of property sold by virtue of delinquency in tax payments.

TAX LIEN — A lien in favor of a taxing authority, and attaching to property on which taxes have not been paid.

TAX ROLL — An official list of all property within a taxing district, showing the tax levied against each property for the current year.

TAX SALE — The sale of property for non-payment of taxes.

TAX SHELTER — An investment that offers an opportunity to reduce or eliminate tax liability, possible because tax-deductible items exceed gross gain.

TENANCY — The temporary use and possession of property owned by another, as in a lease; also used to describe an estate in land, such as tenancy in common, joint tenancy, etc.

TENANCY AT SUFFERANCE	The type of tenancy created where a tenant remains in possession after the expiration of a valid lease and the owner takes no action to remove him.
TENANCY AT WILL	A tenancy which may be terminated by owner or tenant at any time.
TENANCY BY THE ENTIRETY	A form of co-ownership limited to husband and wife, and carrying the right of survivorship. Neither party can individually sell the property.
TENANCY IN COMMON	Property owned by two or more persons who have common possession, but whose titles are separate and distinct. Their respective interests need not be equal, and do not carry the right of survivorship, but descend to the heirs of the respective co-owners.
TENANT	One who holds land.
TERMITE INSPECTION	An inspection for determining the possible presence of termites in a structure.
TERMITE SHIELD	One method of preventing termite infiltration, consisting of a protective covering placed on foundation walls of a structure.
TERM MORTGAGE	A mortgage which does not call for amortization payments. The principal sum is due at the end of the term.
TERM OF LEASE	The period of time a lease is to remain in force.
TESTAMENT	A will. Commonly designated as LAST WILL AND TESTAMENT.
TESTAMENTARY	Having to do with a will.
TESTATE	Leaving a will; a deceased who left a will is said to have died testate. (The opposite of INTESTATE.)
TESTATOR	One who makes a will (the feminine form is TESTATRIX).
"TIME IS OF THE ESSENCE"	This phrase, when used in an agreement, requires that any specified conditions of time or date must be strictly adhered to; any deviation by a party could constitute a breach of contract on his part.
TITLE	Ownership of property; the physical evidence of such ownership.

TITLE CLOSING	In a property sale, the consummation of the transaction, at which time the parties meet, and a deed is delivered in exchange for the purchase price.
TITLE COMPANY	A company engaged in the business of insuring titles.
TITLE INSURANCE	Insurance covering an owner (or mortgagee) against loss caused by defects in title. Also called TITLE POLICY.
TITLE REPORT	A report issued as a result of a title search, describing the condition of the title, usually made by a title insurance company before the issuance of a title insurance policy.
TITLE SEARCH	An examination of the public records to determine the condition of title to property. Normally it will be made either by a title company, preparatory to issuance of a title insurance policy, or by an attorney who will furnish his report to a title insurance company, or to a client (if no insurance is being applied for).
TOPOGRAPHY	The character of the land.
TORRENS SYSTEM	A system of registration of land titles used in some states. The certificate of registration, issued only after certain requirements are met, constitutes a guarantee of the validity of the title, as distinguished from merely recording a deed, which is always subject to legal attack.
TORT	A wrongful act (not necessarily a crime) committed by one against another, other than breach of contract.
TOWNSHIP	In the Rectangular Survey System of land description, an area of 6 square miles, which is further divided into 36 sections of 1 square mile each.
TRADE-IN	A method by which a seller is guaranteed a sale so as to enable him to purchase another property. The broker agrees to purchase the seller's property at a specified discount price if a buyer is not found within a certain period of time.
TRADE NAME	A name other than the family name of the owner, under which a business is conducted.

TRESPASS	To enter upon the land of another without authorization.
TRUST	A legal relationship in which a person (trustee) holds property for the benefit of another (beneficiary or "cestui que trust") pursuant to the directions of the person creating the trust (settlor).
TRUST ACCOUNT	A bank account in which are kept funds held by the depositor for another. Brokers are required to keep client's funds in such an account, separate from the broker's personal account. (Also called ESCROW ACCOUNT or SPECIAL ACCOUNT.)
TRUST DEED	See DEED OF TRUST
TRUSTEE	One who holds property for the benefit of another.
TRUSTOR	In a deed of trust, the one granting title to property as security for a loan; the borrower.
UNDER-IMPROVEMENT	An improvement to property which is not enough to create the "highest and best use" of that property.
UNDISCLOSED PRINCIPAL	One who employs the services of an agent, but whose identity (and perhaps the fact that there is even an agency) is not revealed to third parties.
UNDUE INFLUENCE	The improper taking advantage of another by influencing his mind so that his action does not truly reflect his own wishes. If proved, can be a ground for declaring a contract unenforceable.
UNENFORCEABLE CONTRACT	An agreement valid on its face, but unenforceable by either party because of some circumstance.
UNIFORM COMMERCIAL CODE	A comprehensive statutory code of laws concerning business transactions, designed to give uniformity to the rules in all states. Most states have adopted the code.
UNILATERAL CONTRACT	An agreement calling for an act to be exchanged for a promise. The promise is enforceable against the promisor only upon performance of the act by the promisee.
UNIMPROVED PROPERTY	Land upon which no improvements have been made; vacant land.
UNSECURED LOAN	A loan for which no collateral or security has been posted.

URBAN	Relating to a city or densely populated area, as distinguished from rural or suburban areas.
URBAN RENEWAL	A federal program by which blighted or decayed areas are cleared for the purpose of rebuilding with more desirable structures, particularly low-cost housing.
USURY	Charging a rate of interest higher than allowed by law.
UTILITY VALUE	The extent to which something has usefulness; one of the essential elements in the broad concept of "value."
V.A. LOAN	See V.A. MORTGAGE
V.A. MORTGAGE	A mortgage loan which is partially guaranteed by the Veterans Administration (also called V.A. LOAN, G.I. LOAN, or G.I. MORTGAGE).
VALID	Legally effective and binding; a valid contract is one that is enforceable at law.
VALUABLE CONSIDERATION	Something of material value, paid as a price.
VALUE	Generally, market value—the price a buyer would be willing to pay. In a broader sense, value includes not only the present benefits of property, but the anticipated future benefits as well.
VARIANCE	An exception to the existing zoning requirements, granted to specific property, usually because of some special circumstances.
VENDEE	The purchaser.
VENDOR	The seller.
VERBAL	Oral or spoken; an oral agreement is one not reduced to writing.
VERIFICATION	A sworn statement attesting to the truthfulness of a document.
VERIFY	To swear by executing a verification.
VESTED INTEREST OR RIGHT	An interest or right that is effective and legally enforceable.
VOID	Of no legal force or effect.

VOIDABLE CONTRACT	An agreement that is valid and legally enforceable, but which may be rendered unenforceable by a party; the contract of a minor, for example, is generally voidable by him, with some exceptions.
WAIVE	To give up a right or claim.
WAIVER	A document, or act, by which a right or claim is given up.
WARRANTY	A promise or representation.
WARRANTY DEED	A deed in which the grantor warrants the clarity of the title he is conveying, and promises to defend it against other claimants.
WASTE	The act of depleting the value of real property by someone in temporary possession.
WATER RIGHTS	See RIPARIAN RIGHTS
WATER TABLE	The depth, below the surface of land, at which water is found.
WILL	A document by which one directs the disposition of his assets upon his death; it has no legal effect until such death.
WRAP-AROUND MORTGAGE	A new, increased mortgage which "wraps around" an existing mortgage; a seller, for example, would continue the payments on the existing mortgage, while collecting from a buyer on a larger mortgage at a higher interest rate.
WRIT	A court order commanding someone to perform, or refrain from performing, some act.
WRIT OF EXECUTION	A court order directing an official to seize property of a debtor against whom a judgment has been obtained, the purpose being to sell the property to satisfy the debt.
YIELD	The return on an investment.
ZONING	The control, by regulation, of the use of land.
ZONING BOARD	Also known as ZONING COMMISSION. A group authorized by local government to prepare and implement zoning regulations.
ZONING VARIANCE	See VARIANCE

APPENDIX A

TABLES OF MEASUREMENT

LINEAR MEASURE

12 inches	=	1 foot
3 feet	=	1 yard
16½ feet	=	1 rod or pole
40 rods	=	1 furlong
8 furlongs or 5280 feet	=	1 mile

SQUARE MEASURE

144 square inches	=	1 square foot
9 square feet	=	1 square yard
30¼ square yards	=	1 square rod or square pole
40 square rods	=	1 rood
4 roods or 43,560 square feet	=	1 acre
640 acres	=	1 square mile

CIRCULAR MEASURE

60 seconds (″)	=	1 minute (′)
60 minutes	=	1 degree (°)
90 degrees	=	1 quadrant
4 quadrants (360 degrees)	=	1 circle

APPENDIX B

MONTHLY PAYMENT REQUIRED TO AMORTIZE A $1000 LOAN

Rate of Interest	Length of Term		
	20 years	25 years	30 years
7 %	$ 7.76	$7.07	$6.66
7-¼%	7.91	7.23	6.83
7-½%	8.06	7.39	7.00
7-¾%	8.21	7.56	7.17
8 %	8.37	7.72	7.34
8-¼%	8.53	7.89	7.52
8-½%	8.68	8.06	7.69
8-¾%	8.84	8.23	7.87
9 %	9.00	8.40	8.05
9-¼%	9.16	8.57	8.23
9-½%	9.33	8.74	8.41
9-¾%	9.49	8.92	8.60
10 %	9.66	9.09	8.78
10-½%	10.00	9.45	9.15
11 %	10.33	9.81	9.54

To find the monthly payment, for example, on a $20,000 loan, simply multiply the appropriate figure by 20. (Because of rounding, the total may be off by a few cents).

APPENDIX C

North Carolina Real Estate Brokers Licensing Law

Rules and Regulations, North Carolina Real Estate Licensing Board

CHAPTER 744 OF THE 1957 SESSION LAWS

Codified as Chapter 93A of the General Statutes of North Carolina, entitled "Real Estate Brokers and Salesmen"

SECTION 93A-1. LICENSE REQUIRED OF REAL ESTATE BROKERS AND REAL ESTATE SALESMEN.—From and after July 1, 1957, it shall be unlawful for any person, partnership, association or corporation in this State to act as a real estate broker or real estate salesman, or directly or indirectly to engage or assume to engage in the business of real estate broker or real estate salesman or to advertise or hold himself or themselves out as engaging in or conducting such business without first obtaining a license issued by the North Carolina Real Estate Licensing Board (hereinafter referred to as the Board), under the provisions of this chapter.

SECTION 93A-2. DEFINITIONS AND EXCEPTIONS.—(a) A real estate broker within the meaning of this chapter is any person, partnership, association, or corporation, who for a compensation or valuable consideration or promise thereof lists or offers to list, sells or offers to sell, buys or offers to buy, auctions or offers to auction (specifically not including a mere crier of sales), or negotiates the purchase or sale or exchange of real estate, or who leases or offers to lease, or who sells or offers to sell leases of whatever character, or rents or offers to rent any real estate or the improvement thereon, for others. A broker shall also be deemed to include a person, partnership, association, or corporation who for a fee sells or offers to sell the name or names of persons, partnerships, associations, or corporations who have real estate for rental, lease, or sale.

(b) The term real estate salesman within the meaning of this chapter shall mean and include any person who under the supervision of a real estate broker, for a compensation or valuable consideration is associated with or engaged by or on behalf of a licensed real estate broker to do, perform or deal in any act, acts or transactions set out or comprehended by the foregoing definition of real estate broker.

(c) The provisions of this chapter shall not apply to and shall not include any person, partnership, association or corporation, who, as owner or lessor, shall perform any of the acts aforesaid with reference to property owned or leased by them, where such acts are performed in the regular course of or as an incident to the management of such property and the investment therein; nor shall the provisions of this chapter apply to persons acting as attorney-in-fact under a duly executed power of attorney from the owner authorizing the final consummation of performance of any contract for the sale, lease or exchange of real estate, nor shall this chapter be construed to include in any way the acts or services rendered by an attorney at law; nor shall it be held to include, while acting as such, a receiver, trustee in bankruptcy, guardian, administrator or executor or any such person acting under order of any court, nor to include a trustee acting under a trust agreement, deed of trust or will, or the regular salaried employees thereof, and nothing in this chapter shall be so construed as to require a license for the owner, personally, to sell or lease his own property.

SECTION 93A-3. LICENSING BOARD CREATED; COMPENSATION; ORGANIZATION. — (a) There is hereby created the North Carolina Real Estate Licensing Board for issuing licenses to real estate brokers and real estate salesmen, hereinafter called the Board. The Board shall be composed of five (5) members to be appointed by the Governor: Provided, that two (2) members of said Board shall be a licensed real estate broker or salesman. One member shall be appointed for one year, two for two years and two for three years. Members appointed on the expiration of such term of office shall serve for three years. The members of the Board shall elect one of their members to serve as chairman of the Board. The Governor may remove any member of the Board for misconduct, incompetency, or wilful neglect of duty. The Governor shall have the power to fill all vacancies occurring on said Board.

(b) Members of the Board shall each receive as full compensation for each day accordingly spent on work for the Board, the sum of fifteen dollars ($15.00) per day plus ten dollars ($10.00) per day for subsistence plus travel expense. The total expense of the adminstration of this chapter shall not exceed the total income therefrom; and none of the expenses of said Board or the compensation or expenses of any office thereof or any employee shall ever be paid or payable out of the treasury of the State of North Carolina; and neither the Board nor any officer or employee thereof shall have any power or authority to make or incur any expense, debt or other financial obligation binding upon the State of North Carolina. After all expenses of operation, the Board may set aside an expense reserve each year not to exceed ten per cent (10%) of the previous year's gross income; then any surplus shall go to the general fund of the State of North Carolina.

(c) The Board shall have power to make such bylaws, rules and regulations as it shall deem best, that are not inconsistent with the provisions of this chapter and the laws of North Carolina; provided, however, the Board shall not make rules or regulations regulating commissions, salaries, or fees to be charged by licensees under this chapter. The Board shall adopt a seal for its use, which shall bear thereon the words "North Carolina Real Estate Licensing Board." Copies of all records and papers in the office of the Board duly certified and authenticated by the seal of the Board shall be received in evidence in all courts and with like effect as the originals.

(d) The Board may employ a secretary-treasurer and such clerical assistance as may be necessary to carry out the provisions of this chapter and to put into effect such rules and regulations as the Board may promulgate. The Board shall fix salaries and shall require employees to make good and sufficient surety bonds for the faithful performance of their duties.

(e) The Board shall be entitled to the services of the Attorney General of North Carolina, in connection with the affairs of the Board or may on approval of the Attorney General, employ an attorney to assist or represent it in the enforcement of this chapter, as to specific matters, but the fee paid for such service shall be approved by the Attorney General. The Board may prefer a complaint for violation of this chapter before any court of competent jurisdiction, and it may take the necessary legal steps through the proper legal offices of the State to enforce the provisions of this chapter and collect the penalties provided therein.

(f) The Board is authorized to expend expense reserve funds as defined in G.S. 93A-3(b) for the purpose of conducting education and information programs relating to the real estate brokerage business for the information, education, guidance and protection of the general public, licensees, and applicants for license. The education and information programs may include preparation, printing and distribution of publications and articles and the conduct of conferences, seminars, and lectures.

SECTION 93A-4. APPLICATIONS FOR LICENSES; FEES; QUALIFICATIONS; EXAMINATIONS: PRIVILEGE-LICENSES; RENEWAL OR REINSTATEMENT OF LICENSE; POWER TO ENFORCE PROVISIONS.—(a) Any person, partnership, association, or corporation hereafter desiring to enter into business of and obtain a license as a real estate broker or real estate salesman shall make written application for such license to the Board on such forms as are prescribed by the Board. Each applicant for a license as a real estate broker shall be a citizen of the United States and shall be at least 21 years of age. Each applicant for a license as a real estate broker shall have been actively engaged as a licensed real estate salesman in this State for at least 12 months prior to making application for a license as a real estate broker, or shall furnish evidence satisfactory to the Board of experience in real estate transactions which the Board shall find equivalent to such 12 months experience as a licensed real estate salesman, or shall furnish evidence satisfactory to the Board of completion of 30 classroom hours of such courses of education in real estate subjects at a school approved by the Board as the Board shall by regulation prescribe. Each applicant for a license as a real estate salesman shall furnish evidence satisfactory to the Board of completion of 30 classroom hours of such courses of education in real estate subjects at a school approved by the Board as the Board shall by regulation prescribe or shall furnish evidence satisfactory to the Board of experience in real estate transactions which the Board shall find equivalent to such real estate education. Each application for a license as real estate broker shall be accompanied by twenty-five dollars ($25.00). Each application for license as a real estate salesman shall be accompanied by fifteen dollars ($15.00), and shall state the name and address of the real estate broker with whom the applicant is to be associated.

(NOTE: A 1974 amendment to G.S. 93B provides that "no occupational licensing board may require that an individual be more than 18 years of age as a requirement for receiving a license.")

(b) Any person who files such application to the Board in proper manner for a license as real estate broker or a license as real estate salesman shall be required to take an oral or written examination to determine his qualifications with due regard to the paramount interests of the public as to the honesty, truthfulness, integrity and competency of the applicant. If the results of the examination shall be satisfactory to the Board, then the Board shall issue to such a person a license, authorizing such person to act as a real estate broker or real estate salesman in the State of North Carolina, upon the payment of privilege taxes now required by law or that may hereafter be required by law. Anyone failing to pass an examination may be re-examined without payment of additional fees, under such rules as the Board may adopt in such cases.

Provided, however, that any person who, at the time of the passage or at the effective date of this chapter, has a license to engage in, and is engaged in business as a real estate broker or real estate salesman and who shall file a sworn application with the Board setting forth his qualifications, including a statement that such applicant has not within 5 years preceding the filing of the application been convicted of any felony or any misdemeanor involving moral turpitude, shall not be required to take or pass such examination, but all such persons shall be entitled to receive such license from the Board under the provisions of this chapter on proper application therefor and payment of a fee of ten dollars ($10.00).

(c) All licenses granted and issued by the Board under the provisions of this chapter shall expire on the 30th day of June following issuance thereof, and shall become invalid after such date unless reinstated. Renewal of such license may be effected at any time during the month of June preceding the date of expiration of such license upon proper application to the Board accompanied by the payment of a renewal fee of ten dollars ($10.00) to the secretary-treasurer of the Board, **[provided, the Board may by regulation require the renewal of such licenses for periods not exceeding three years upon payment of a renewal fee of ten dollars ($10.00) for each twelve-month period; provided further, that in the event of the licensee's death, removal to another state or upon voluntary**

surrender of the renewed license the Board shall, upon written application by the licensee or his estate, (administrator, executor, or personal representative) refund the amount of the renewal fee prepaid for the unexpired license year or years other than the current year and the renewal receipt or pocket card shall contain notice of this refund provision. Effective January 1, 1976.] All licenses reinstated after the expiration date thereof shall be subject to a late filing fee of five dollars ($5.00) in addition to the required renewal fee. In the event a licensee fails to obtain a reinstatement of such license within twelve months after the expiration date thereof, the Board may, in its discretion, consider such person as not having been previously licensed, and thereby subject to the provisions of this chapter relating to the issuance of an original license, including the examination requirements set forth herein. Duplicate licenses may be issued by the Board upon payment of a fee of one dollar ($1.00) by the licensee.

(d) The board is expressly vested with the power and authority to make and enforce any and all such reasonable rules and regulations connected with the application for any license as shall be deemed necessary to administer and enforce the provisions of this chapter.

(e) Nothing contained in this chapter shall be construed as giving any authority to the Board nor any licensee of the Board as authorizing any licensee whether by examination or under the grandfather clause or by comity to engage in the practice of law or to render any legal service as specifically set out in G.S. 84-2.1 or any other legal service not specifically referred to in said section.

SECTION 93A-5. REGISTER OF APPLICANTS; ROSTER OF BROKERS AND SALESMEN; FINANCIAL REPORT TO SECRETARY OF STATE.—(a) The secretary-treasurer of the Board shall keep a register of all applicants for license, showing for each the date of application, name, place of business, place of residence, and whether the license was granted or refused. Said register shall be prima facie evidence of all matters recorded therein.

(b) The secretary-treasurer of the Board shall also keep a current roster showing the names and places of business of all licensed real estate brokers and real estate salesmen, which roster shall be kept on file in the office of the Board and be open to public inspection.

(c) On or before the first day of September of each year, the Board shall file with the Secretary of State a copy of the roster of real estate brokers and real estate salesmen holding certificates of license, and at the same time shall also file with the Secretary of State a report containing a complete statement of receipts and disbursements of the Board for the preceding fiscal year ending June 30th attested by the affidavit of the secretary-treasurer of the Board.

SECTION 93A-6. REVOCATION OR SUSPENSION OF LICENSES BY BOARD.—(a) The Board shall have power to revoke or suspend licenses as herein provided. The Board may upon its own motion, and shall upon the verified complaint in writing of any persons, provided such complaint with the evidence, documentary or otherwise, presented in connection therewith, shall make out a prima facie case, hold a hearing as hereinafter provided and investigate the actions of any real estate broker or real estate salesman, or any person who shall assume to act in either such capacity, and shall have power to suspend or revoke any license issued under the provisions of this chapter at any time where the licensee has by false or fraudulent representations obtained a license or has been convicted or has entered a plea of nolo contendere upon which a finding of guilty and final judgment has been entered in a court of competent jurisdiction in this State or in any other state of the criminal offense of embezzlement, obtaining money under false pretenses, forgery, conspiracy to defraud or any similar offense of offenses involving moral turpitude or where the licensee in performing or attempting to perform any of the acts mentioned herein is deemed to be guilty of:

(1) Making any substantial and willful misrepresentations, or,

(2) Making any false promises of a character likely to influence, persuade, or induce, or

(3) Pursuing a course of misrepresentation or making of false promises through agents or salesmen or advertising or otherwise, or

(4) Acting for more than one party in a transaction without the knowledge of all parties for whom he acts, or

(5) Accepting a commission or valuable consideration as a real estate salesman for the performances of any of the acts specified in this chapter, from any person, except the licensed broker by whom he is employed, or

(6) Representing or attempting to represent a real estate broker other than the broker by whom he is engaged or associated, without the express knowledge and consent of the broker with whom he is associated, or

(7) Failing, within a reasonable time, to account for or to remit any moneys coming into his possession which belong to others, or

(8) Being unworthy or incompetent to act as a real estate broker or salesman in such manner as to safeguard the interests of the public, or

(9) Paying a commission or valuable consideration to any person for acts or services performed in violation of this chapter, or

(10) Any other conduct whether of the same or a different character from that hereinbefore specified which constitutes improper, fraudulent or dishonest dealing.

(11) For performing or undertaking to perform any legal service as set forth in G.S. 84-2.1 or any other such acts not specifically set forth in said section.

(12) Commingling the money or other property of his principals with his own or failure to maintain and deposit in a trust or escrow account in an insured bank or savings and loan assocation in North Carolina all money received by a real estate broker acting in said capacity, or as escrow agent, or the temporary custodian of the funds of others, in a real estate transaction; provided, such accounts shall not bear interest unless the principals authorize in writing the deposit be made in an interest bearing account and also provide for the disbursement of the interest thereon.

(13) Failure to deliver, within a reasonable time, a completed copy of any purchase agreement or offer to buy and sell real estate to the buyer and to the seller.

(14) Failure by a broker to deliver to the seller in every real estate transaction wherein he acts as a real estate broker, at the time such transaction is consummated, a complete detailed closing statement showing all of the receipts and disbursements handled by such broker for the seller; also failure to deliver to the buyer a complete statement showing all money received in the transaction from such buyer and how and for what the same were disbursed.

(15) Violating any rule or regulation duly promulgated by the board.

(b) In all proceedings under this section for the revocation or suspension of licenses, the provisions of Chapter 150A of the General Statutes shall be applicable.

(c) Records relative to the deposit, maintenance, and withdrawal of the money or other property of his principals shall be properly maintained by a broker and made available to the Board or its authorized representative when the Board determines such records are pertinent to the conduct of the investigation of any specific complaint against a licensee.

SECTION 93A-7. POWER OF COURTS TO REVOKE.—Whenever any person, partnership, association or corporation claiming to have been injured or damaged by the gross negligence, incompetency, fraud, dishonesty or misconduct on the part of any licensee following the calling or engaging in the business herein described and shall file suit upon such claim against such licensee in any court of record in this State and shall recover judgment thereon, such court may as part of its judgment or decree in such case, if it deem it a proper case in which so to do, order a written copy of the transcript of record in said case to be forwarded by the clerk of court to the chairman of the said Board with a recommendation that the licensee's certificate of license be revoked.

SECTION 93-8. PENALTY FOR VIOLATION OF CHAPTER.—Any person violating the provisions of this chapter shall upon conviction thereof be deemed guilty of a misdemeanor and shall be punished by a fine or imprisonment, or by both fine and imprisonment, in the discretion of the court.

SECTION 93A-9. LICENSING NONRESIDENTS.—An applicant from another state, which offers licensing privileges to residents of North Carolina, may be licensed by conforming to all the provisions of this Chapter and, in the discretion of the Board, such other terms and conditions as are required of North Carolina residents applying for license in such other state; provided that the Board may exempt from the examination prescribed in G.S. 93A-4 a broker or salesman duly licensed in another state if a similar exemption is extended to licensed brokers and salesmen from North Carolina.

SECTION 93A-10. NONRESIDENT LICENSEES; FILING OF CONSENT AS TO SERVICE OF PROCESS AND PLEADINGS.—Every nonresident applicant shall file an irrevocable consent that suits and actions may be commenced against such applicant in any of the courts of record of this State, by the service of any process or pleading authorized by the laws of this State in any county in which the plaintiff may reside, by serving the same on the secretary of the commission, said consent stipulating and agreeing that such service of such process or pleadings on said secretary shall be taken and held in all courts to be valid and binding as if due service had been made personally upon the applicant in this State. This consent shall be duly acknowledged, and, if made by a corporation, shall be authenticated by its seal. An application from a corporation shall be accompanied by a duly certified copy of the resolution of the board of directors, authorizing the proper officers to execute it. In all cases where process or pleadings shall be served, under the provisions of this chapter, upon the secretary of the commission, such process or pleadings shall be served in duplicate, one of which shall be filed in the office of the commission and the other shall be forewarded immediately by the secretary of the commission, by registered mail, to the last known business address of the nonresident licensee against which such process or pleadings are directed.

SECTION 93A-11. CONSTITUTIONALITY.—That if any Section, subsection, sentence or clause of this Act is for any reason held to be unconstitutional, such holding or decision shall not affect any other portion of the Act, it being declared the legislative intent that this Act would have been enacted notwithstanding such invalid portion.

SECTION 93A-12. All laws and clauses of laws in conflict with this Act are hereby repealed.

SECTION 93A-13. This Act shall be in full force and effect on the 1st day of July, 1957.

In the General Assembly read three times and ratified, this the 21st day of May, 1957.

NORTH CAROLINA ADMINISTRATIVE CODE
TITLE 21
OCCUPATIONAL LICENSING BOARDS
CHAPTER 58
REAL ESTATE LICENSING BOARD
SECTION .0100 —
GENERAL BROKERAGE

.0101 Display of License

The license of a broker and the license of each broker and salesman in his employ or under his supervision shall be prominently displayed at the broker's business address.

History Note: Statutory Authority G.S. 93A-3(c);
Eff. February 1, 1976.

0102 Branch Office

In addition to his principal place of business, a licensed broker may maintain one or more branch offices under the same business name at different locations. A licensed broker who maintains a branch office 50 or more miles from such broker's principal office must employ a licensed real estate broker to actively manage such office and to supervise the real estate salesmen working from such branch office; the license of the broker employed to actively manage such branch office shall be displayed in the branch office.

History Note: Statutory Authority G.S. 93A-3(c);
Eff. February 1, 1976.

.0103 Change of Address or Business Name

All licensees shall notify the Board in writing of each change of residence and business address and each change of business or trade name within 10 days of said change. Addresses shall set forth street name and house numbers in addition to the Post Office Box number (if Post Office Box is listed) for street addresses, and street or highway address, route number and box number for all rural addresses.

History Note: Statutory Authority G.S. 93A-3(c);
Eff. February 1, 1976.

.0104 Listing Contracts

Every written listing contract shall provide for its existence for a definite period of time and for its termination without prior notice at the expiration of that period. It shall not require an owner to notify a broker of his intention to terminate the listing.

History Note: Statutory Authority G.S. 93A-3(c);
Eff. February 1, 1976.

.0105 Advertising

(a) Blind Ads. A broker shall not advertise the sale, purchase, exchange, rent or lease of real estate, for another or others, in a manner indicating the offer to sell, purchase, exchange, or lease is being made by a principal. Every such advertisement shall clearly indicate that it is the advertisement of a broker or brokerage firm and shall not be confined to publication of only a post office box number, telephone number, or street address.

(b) Registration of Assumed Name. In the event that any licensee shall advertise in any manner using a firm name, corporate name, or an assumed name which does not set form the surname of the licensee, he shall first notify the Board in writing of such name or names and furnish the Board with a copy of each certificate filed with the office of the Country Register of Deeds in compliance with Secton 66-68, North Carolina General Statutes.

(c) Authority to Advertise:

> (1) A salesman shall not advertise the sale, purchase, exchange, rent or lease of real estate for another or others without his broker's consent and without including in the advertisement the name of the broker and firm with whom he is associated.

> (2) A broker shall not display a "For Sale" or "For Rent" sign on any real estate without the consent of the owner or his authorized agent.

History Note: Statutory Authority G.S. 93A-3(c);
>   Eff. February 1, 1976.

.0106 Delivery of Instruments

Every real estate broker or real estate salesman shall immediately, but in no event later than five days from the date of execution, deliver to the parties thereto copies of any contract, offer, lease, or option affecting real property.

History Note: Statutory Authority G.S. 93A-3(c);
>   Eff. February 1, 1976.

.0107 Handling and Accounting of Funds

(a) All monies received by a real estate broker acting in his fiduciary capacity shall be deposited in a trust or escrow account within 72 hours of receipt. All monies received by a real estate salesman shall be delivered immediately to the broker by whom he is employed.

(b) Closing statements shall be furnished to the buyer and the seller in the transaction at the closing or not more than five days after closing.

History Note: Statutory Authority G.S. 93A-3(c)
>   Eff. February 1, 1976.

.0108 Retention of Records

Real estate brokers shall retain records of all transactions conducted in such capacity for a period of three years. Such records shall include contracts of sale, written leases, listing contracts, options, offers to purchase, trust records, earnest money receipts, closing statements and any other records pertaining to real estate transactions.

History Note: Statutory Authority G.S. 93A-3(c);

Eff. February 1, 1976.

.0109 Brokerage Commission Disputes

The Board is not a board of arbitration and has no jurisdiction to settle disputes between parties concerning such matters of contract as the rate of commissions, the division of commissions, pay of salesmen, and similar matters. The Board recommends, to avoid differences between parties, that all agreements concerning real estate transfers be reduced to writing at the earliest practical times.

History Note: Statutory Authority G.S. 93A-3(c);

Eff. February 1, 1976

SECTION .0200 —
GENERAL PROVISIONS

.0201 Definitions

As used in this chapter:

(1) "Board" shall mean the North Carolina Real Estate Licensing Board;

(2) "Licensing law" shall refer to Chapter 93A, General Statutes of North Carolina;

(3) "Secretary-Treasurer" shall refer to the Secretary-Treasurer of the Board.

History Note: Statutory Authority G.S. 93A-3(c);

Eff. February 1, 1976.

.0202 Board; Description; Offices

The Board is composed of five members appointed by the Governor pursuant to Section 93A-3, North Carolina General Statutes. It conducts business through a Secretary-Treasurer who employs an assistant and other clerical staff. Offices are located at Room 813, Branch Bank and Trust Building, 333 Fayetteville Street, Raleigh, North Carolina. Office hours are 8:00 a.m. until 5:00 p.m. Monday through Friday, except holidays.

History Note: Statutory Authority G.S. 93A-3(a),(c),(d);

Eff. February 1, 1976.

.0203 Mailing Address

Correspondence by mail should be addressed to the Board at P.O. Box 266, Raleigh, North Carolina 27602.

History Note: Statutory Authority G.S. 93A-3(c);

Eff. February 1, 1976.

.0204 Purpose

It is the responsibility of the Board to license real estate brokers and salesmen and to see that the qualifications and activities of real estate brokers and salesmen are in accord with law and in the best interests of the public.

History Note: Statutory Authority G.S. 93A-3(a),(c);

Eff. February 1, 1976.

SECTION .0300 —
APPLICATION FOR LICENSE

.0301 Form

Any person desiring to obtain a license as real estate broker or salesman shall make written application to the Board upon a prescribed form. Such forms are available upon request to the Board. In general, the form calls for information such as the applicant's name and address, a recent passport size photograph of the applicant, past and present places of residence, education, prior real estate licenses, prior arrests and convictions, unpaid judgments, endorsements of good character by two persons, and whether application is based upon successful completion of an approved real estate course or upon experience.

History Note: Statutory Authority G.S.93A-3(c); 93A-4(a),(d); 150A-11;

Eff. February 1, 1976.

.0302 Filing and Fees

(a) Properly completed applications must be filed (received—not post-marked) in the Board's office on or before the filing date established by the Board for a scheduled examination and must be accompanied by the appropriate fee. Once the application has been filed and processed, the application fee will not be refunded.

(b) The following fees shall be charged:

Application for new broker license $25.00

Application for new salesman license $15.00

History Note: Statutory Authority G.S. 93A-3(c); 93A-4(a),(d);

Eff. February 1, 1976.

.0303 Payment of Application Fees

Payment of application fees shall be made by certified check or money order payable to the North Carolina Real Estate Licensing Board.

History Note: Statutory Authority G.S. 93A-3(c); 93A-4(a),(d);

Eff. February 1, 1976.

SECTION .0400 —
EXAMINATIONS

.0401 Time and Place

Examinations for broker's and salesman's licenses will be scheduled at such times and places as determined by the Secretary-Treasurer. Applicants will be given written notice of when and where to appear for examination.

History Note: Statutory Authority G.S. 93A-3(c); 93A-4(b),(d);

Eff. February 1, 1976.

.0402 Subject Matter

The examination shall test the applicant's knowledge of the following requried subjects:

(1) a practical and working knowledge of the real estate business, including fundamentals of real estate, real estate finance, real estate brokerage, real estate appraising, real property law and mechanics of closing;

(2) the provisions of the licensing law;

(3) the rules and regulations of the Board.

History Note: Statutory Authority G.S. 93A-3(c); 93A-4(b),(d);

Eff. February 1, 1976.

.0403 Re-examination

If the applicant does not appear at the initial examination for which he has been scheduled or fails to pass such examination, he will be re-scheduled for the examination held two months later, except that no examination will be scheduled for December. If he again does not appear or fails to pass this examination, he shall file a complete new application and fee, if he wishes to continue.

History Note: Statutory Authority G.S. 93A-3(c); 93A-4(b),(d);

Eff. February 1, 1976.

**SECTION .0500 —
LICENSING**

.0501 Character

(a) At a meeting of the Board following each examination, the applicants who have passed the examination shall be considered for licensing. The Board will consider any information before it, including references with respect to the paramount interests of the public as to the honesty, truthfulness, and integrity of the applicant prior to granting a license. In the event the information is not adequate for determination, the Board may request additional references or information from an applicant or conduct a careful inquiry into each case in which it appears that the applicant has operated or may have operated in violation of the licensing law. Action of the Board will be deferred until it affirmatively appears that the applicant is possessed of the requisite truth, honesty and integrity.

(b) Every applicant shall have the burden of proving that he is possessed of the requisite truth, honesty and integrity and that he is entitled to the high regard and confidence of the public.

History Note: Statutory Authority G.S. 93A-3(c); 93A-4(b),(d); 150A-11;

Eff. February 1, 1976.

.0502 Corporations

(a) Corporations required to be licensed as real estate broker shall make written application to the Board upon prescribed forms. These forms are available upon request to the Board and call for such information as the corporate name, the address of its principal office, evidence of authority under its corporate charter to engage in the business of real estate brokerage, resolution by the board of directors authorizing the application, past convictions of criminal offenses of any corporate director or officer and a list of all brokers and salesmen associated with the corporation.

(b) A foreign corporation shall further qualify by filing, with its application for license, a copy of its certificate of authority to transact business in this state issued by the North Carolian Secretary of State in accordance with Section 55-131, North Carolina General Statutes, and a Consent to Service of process and pleadings which shall be authenticated by its corporate seal and accompanied by a duly certified copy of the resolution of the board of directors authorizing the proper officer or officers to execute said Consent.

(c) After filing of written application with the Board and upon a showing that at least one executive officer of said corporation holds a current broker's license in good standing, the corporation will be licensed provided it appears that the applicant corporation employs and is directed by personnel possessed of requisite truth, honesty and integrity.

(d) The licensing of a corporation shall not be construed to extend to the licensing of its officers and employees in their individual capacities regardless of whether they are engaged in furthering the business of the licensed corporation.

History Note: Statutory Authority G.S. 93A-3(c); 93A-4(b),(d); 150A-11;
Eff. February 1, 1976.

.0503 License Renewal; Penalty for Non-Renewal

(a) Any licensee desiring the renewal of a license in good standing shall apply for same in writing upon a form approved by the Board during the month of June and shall forward the required fee of $10.00. Forms are available upon request to the Board.

(b) Any person who engages in the business of real estate broker or real estate salesman while his license is lapsed will be subject to the penalties prescribed in the licensing law.

History Note: Statutory Authority G.S. 93A-3(c); 93A-4(c),(d); 150A-11;
Eff. February 1, 1976.

.0504 Inactive License Status

(a) A real estate broker or salesman may return his license to the Board and have such license placed on an inactive status. Inactive licenses may be renewed upon the payment of the regular $10.00 annual renewal fee and, if so renewed, may be reactivated at any time within three years following placement on inactive status without re-examination by making written request to the Board and paying $1.00 fee for re-issuance of license.

(b) In the event a license has been on inactive status for a continuous period of more than three years, the Board may, in its discretion, subject the holder of such license to the requirements of an original applicant.

(c) The holder of an inactive license shall not be entitled to act in any capacity for which a license is required until his license has been reactivated.

Inactive licenses may be revoked or suspended by the Board when conditions exist under which an active license could be revoked or suspended.

History Note: Statutory Authority G.S. 93A-3(c); 93A-4(d); 150A-11;
Eff. February 1, 1976.

.0505 Expired License

Expired licenses may be reinstated within 12 months after expiration upon proper application and payment of the $10.00 renewal fee plus $5.00 late filing fee. Licenses expired for more than 12 months may be considered for reinstatement upon proper application and payment of $25.00 fee for brokers and $15.00 fee for salesmen. Such applications will be reviewed by the Board to determine whether an examination will be required.

History Note: Statutory Authority G.S. 93A-3(c); 93A-4(c)(d); 150A-11;
Eff. February 1, 1976.

.0506 Salesman to be Associated with and Supervised by Broker

A salesman's license is valid only while he is associated with and supervised by a broker. Upon termination of such association, the broker shall immediately endorse the back of the salesman's license, showing date of termination, and return same to the Board for inactive status or transfer. The salesman concerned may have his license re-issued and transferred to a new broker by filing a prescribed transfer form with $1.00 fee. These forms are available upon request to the Board.

History Note: Statutory Authority G.S. 93A-2(b); 93A-3(c); 150A-11;
Eff. February 1, 1976.

.0507 Payment of License Fees

Checks given the Board in payment of license fees which are returned unpaid shall be considered cause for license denial, suspension, or revocation. Checks drawn on escrow or trust accounts are not acceptable for payment of license fees.

History Note: Statutory Authority G.S. 93A-3(c); 94A-4(c),(d); 150A-11;
Eff. February 1, 1976.

.0508 Duplicate License Fee

A duplicate license may be issued due to loss or destruction of an original license upon payment of a $1.00 fee.

History Note: Statutory Authority G.S. 93A-3(c); 93A-4(c),(d); 150A-11;
Eff. February 1, 1976.

SECTION .0600 —
ADMINISTRATIVE HEARINGS

.0601 Form and Preparation of Complaints

The board may investigate complaints and assist in the preparation of written and verified complaints. Information which does not set forth the name and address of the informant will be disregarded. Complaint forms are available upon request to the Board.

History Note: Statutory Authority G.S. 93A-3(c); 93A-6(a); 150A-11;
Eff. February 1, 1976.

.0602 Prima Facie Case

Whenever it shall be made to appear upon the written and verified complaint of any person that any licensee under the Act has been guilty of a violation of Section 93A-6, North Carolina General Statutes, or any subsection or subsections thereof, or of any of these rules and regulations of the Board, and further by the same complaint or by additional affidavits or other documentary evidence that a prima facie case of a violation exists, the Board will hold a public hearing in accordance with the provisions of Chapter 150A of the General Statutes.

History Note: Statutory Authority G.S. 93A-3(c); 93A-6(a); 150A-11;
Eff. February 1, 1976.

.0603 Request for Hearing

An individual who is entitled to an administrative hearing and who has not received notice of a right to hearing, may file a request for a hearing with the Board. The Secretary-Treasurer, under the direction of the Board, will decide whether to grant the request.

History Note: Statutory Authority G.S. 93A-3(c); 150A-11; 150A-23.
Eff. February 1, 1976.

.0604 Notice of Hearing

In addition to the items specified in Section 150A-23, North Carolina General Statutes, notices of administrative hearings:
  (1) shall include a statement that failure to inform the Board, within the time specified in the notice, of intent to appear at a hearing will be deemed a waiver of the right to a hearing;
  (2) may schedule the date of hearing;
  (3) may include any other information deemed relevant to informing the party as to the procedure of the hearing.

History Note: Statutory Authority G.S. 93A-3(c); 150A-11; 150A-23;
Eff. February 1, 1976.

.0605 Who Shall Hear Contested Cases

Administrative hearings will be heard by any or all of the Board members or a designated hearing officer or officers.

History Note: Statutory Authority G.S. 93A-3(c); 150A-32;
Eff. February 1, 1976.

.0606 Failure to Appear

Should a party fail to appear at a scheduled hearing, the Board members or hearing officer may proceed with the hearing in the party's absence, or may order a continuance, adjournment or like disposition, or may dismiss the proceeding.

History Note: Statutory Authority G.S. 93A-3(c); 150A-11; 150A-25(a);
   Eff. February 1, 1976.

.0607 Petition to Reopen Proceeding

(a) If a hearing is conducted or a decision is reached in the absence of a party, that party may file a written petition with the Board to reopen the case.

(b) Petitions to reopen a case will not be granted except when the petitioner can show that his absence was unavoidable and that fairness requires reopening the case. Upon the running of the 30 day period for seeking judicial review, such petitions will have no effect.

(c) The decision whether to grant a petition to reopen a case is within the discretion of the Board or its designate.

History Note: Statutory Authority G.S. 93A-3(c); 150A-11; 150A-25;
   Eff. February 1, 1976.

.0608 Answer

A party who has been served with a notice of hearing may file a written answer with the Secretary-Treasurer not later than seven days before the date for hearing.

History Note: Statutory Authority G.S. 93A-3(c); 150A-11; 150A-25(b)
   Eff. February 1, 1976.

.0609 Intervention

A person desiring to intervene in a hearing must file a petition to intervene as provided in Section 1A-1, Rule 24, North Carolina General Statutes. The petition must be made upon a form supplied by the Board. This form calls for such information as the claim or defense for which intervention is sought and the grounds therefor. All such petitions shall be filed with the Secretary-Treasurer who, upon direction of the Board, will decide with reasonable promptness whether to allow the petition.

History Note: Statutory Authority G.S. 93A-3(c); 150A-11; 150A-23(d);
   Eff. February 1, 1976.

.0610 Subpoenas

(a) The Secretary-Treasurer is delegated the power to issue subpoenas in the Board's name.

(b) Subpoenas requiring the attendance of witnesses, or those to produce documents, evidence, or other things, will be issued promptly by the Secretary-Treasurer after receipt of a request from a party for such subpoena, except as stated below.

(c) The Secretary-Treasurer will have the discretion to refuse a request for the issuance of a subpoena, if clearly, on its face, the request is objectionable or unreasonable.

(d) Except as may be otherwise stated in a particular subpoena, any person receiving a subpoena may object thereto by filing a written objection with the Secretary-Treasurer. Such objections shall contain a concise but complete statement of the reasons why the subpoena should be revoked or modified. The objecting witness shall serve his objection on the party who requested the subpoena as soon as he files the objection with the Secretary-Treasurer.

(e) Upon notification to all concerned parties and as soon as practical, the Secretary-Treasurer may hear evidence and any arguments relating to issuance of a subpoena. The Secretary-Treasurer will rule on the challenge and issue a decision.

History Note: Statutory Authority G.S. 93A-3(c); 150A-11; 150A-27;
Eff. February 1, 1976.

SECTION .0700 —
PETITIONS FOR RULES

.0701 Petition for Rule Making Hearings

(a) Any person wishing to file a petition requesting the adoption, amendment or repeal of a rule by the Board shall address a petition to the Secretary-Treasurer.

(b) The petition shall include the following information:

(1) name(s), address(es) and occupation(s) of petitioner(s);

(2) an indication of the subject area to which the petition is directed;

(3) either a draft of the proposed rule or a summary of its contents;

(4) reasons for the proposal;

(5) the effect on existing rules or orders;

(6) the effect on existing practices in the area involved, including costs;

(7) any data supporting the proposal;

(8) names of those most likely to be affected by the proposed rule.

History Note: Statutory Authority G.S. 93A-3(c); 150A-16;
Eff. February 1, 1976.

.0702 Disposition of Petitions

(a) The Secretary-Treasurer will determine whether the public interest will be served by granting the request. Prior to making this determination, the Secretary-Treasurer may request additional information from the petitioner(s) and may use any other appropriate method for obtaining information on which to base his determination.

(b) Within 30 days of submission of the petition, a final decision will be rendered by the Secretary-Treasurer. If the decision is to deny the petition, the Secretary-Treasurer will notify the petitioner in writing, stating the reasons for denial. If the decision is to grant the petition, the Secretary-Treasurer will initiate a rule making proceeding and give at least 10 days notice to interested persons of a public hearing on the proposed rule as the circumstances permit.

History Note: Statutory Authority G.S. 93A-3(c); 150A-16;
Eff. February 1, 1976.

.0703 Additional Information

Persons desiring information in addition to that contained in a rule making notice may write to the Board, indicating clearly the rule making proceeding which is the subject of the inquiry.

History Note: Statutory Authority G.S. 93A-3(c); 150A-12;

Eff. February 1, 1976.

SECTION .0800 —
RULE MAKING

.0801 Request to Participate

Any person desiring to present oral data, views, or arguments on a proposed rule must, at least five days prior to the hearing, file a notice with the Board. Such notice must contain a clear reference to the proposed rule, a brief summary of the individual's views in respect thereto, and how long the individual desires to speak.

History Note: Statutory Authority G.S. 93A-3(c); 150A-11; 150A-12(e);

Eff. February 1, 1976.

.0802 Written Submissions

Any person may file a written submission containing data, comments or arguments, after publication of a rule making notice and within 10 days after the hearing. Written submissions should be addressed to the Board and should clearly state the rule or proposed rule to which the comments are directed.

History Note: Statutory Authority G.S. 93A-3(c); 150A-11; 150A-12(e);

Eff. February 1, 1976.

.0803 Presiding Officer; Powers and Duties

The presiding officer at the hearing shall have complete control of the proceedings, including: extensions of any time requirements, recognition of speakers, time allotments for presentations, the right to question speakers, direction of the discussion, and management of the hearing.

History Note: Statutory Authority G.S. 93A-3(c); 150A-11; 150A-12(a),(d);

Eff. February 1, 1976.

.0804 Statement of Reasons for Decision

(a) Any interested person desiring a concise statement of the principal reasons for and against the adoption of a rule by the Board and the factors that led to overruling the considerations urged against its adaption, may submit a request to the Secretary-Treasurer.

(b) The request must be made in writing and submitted prior to adoption of the rule or within 30 days thereafter.

History Note: Statutory Authority G.S. 93A-3(c); 150A-11; 150A-12(e);

Eff. February 1, 1976.

.0805 Record of Proceedings

A record of rule making proceedings will be available for public inspection during regular office hours at the Board's office. This record will contain the original petition, the notice, all written memoranda and information submitted, and a record or summary of oral presentations, if any.

History Note: Statutory Authority G.S. 93A-3(c); 150A-11;
Eff. February 1, 1976.

SECTION .0900 —
DECLARATORY HEARINGS

.0901 Subjects of Declaratory Rulings

Any person substantially affected by a statute administered or rule promulgated by the Board, may request a declaratory ruling as to either the manner in which a statute or rule applies to a given factual situation, if at all, or whether a particular Board rule is valid.

History Note: Statutory Authority G.S. 93A-3(c); 150A-17;
Eff. February 1, 1976.

.0902 Submission of Request for Ruling

All requests for declaratory rulings shall be written and mailed to the Board. The request must contain the following information:

(1) name, address, telephone number, and signature of petitioner;
(2) statute or rule to which the petition relates;
(3) concise statement of the manner in which petitioner is aggrieved by the rule or statute or its potential application to him;
(4) statement of the interpretation given the statute or rule in question by petitioner;
(5) statement of the reasons, including any legal authorities, in support of the interpretation given the statute or rule by petitioner.

History Note: Statutory Authority G.S. 93A-3(c); 150A-17;
Eff. February 1, 1976.

.0903 Disposition of Requests

The Board will, with reasonable promptness, either deny the requests, stating the reasons therefor, or issue a declaratory ruling. Whenever the Board believes for good cause that the issuance of a declaratory ruling is undesirable, it may refuse to issue such ruling. The Board will ordinarily refuse to issue a declaratory ruling:

(1) unless the petitioner shows that the circumstances are so changed since the adoption of the rule that such a ruling would be warranted;
(2) unless the petitioner shows that the Board did not give full consideration to the factors specified in the request for a declaratory ruling at the time the rule was issued;
(3) where there has been a similar controlling factual determination in a

contested case, or where the factual context being raised for a declaratory ruling was specifically considered upon the adoption of the rule or directive being questioned;
  (4) where the subject matter of the request is involved in pending litigation in any state or federal court in North Carolina or in a pending administrative hearing.
History Note: Statutory Authority G.S. 93A-3(c); 150A-17;
    Eff. February 1, 1976.

.0904 Applicability of Ruling
A declaratory ruling shall be applicable only to the factual situation alleged in the petition or request. It shall not be applicable to different factual situations or where additional facts, not considered in the ruling, exist.
History Note: Statutory Authority G.S. 93A-3(c); 150A-17;
    Eff. February 1, 1976.

.0905 Record of Ruling
A record of all declaratory rule making proceedings will be maintained at the Board's office and will be available for public inspection during regular office hours.
History Note: Statutory Authority G.S. 93A-4(c); 150A-11;
    Eff. February 1, 1976.

SECTION .1000 —
REAL ESTATE SCHOOLS

.1001 Application for Course Approval
Schools seeking approval of their course shall file an application with the Board on the official stationery of the school. The application shall include the following information:
  (1) the name and address of the school;
  (2) location where classes will be held;
  (3) dates that course begins and ends;
  (4) number of classroom hours and subjects covered in the course;
  (5) names of textbooks used in the course.
History Note: Statutory Authority G.S.93A-4(a);
    Eff. February 1, 1976.

.1002 Private Schools; Evidence of License
Private schools shall furnish, with their application for Board approval, evidence that they are licensed by the North Carolina Board of Education in accordance with Article 31, Chapter 115, of the North Carolina General Statutes.
History Note: Statutory Authority G.S. 93A-4(a);
    Eff. February 1, 1976.

.1003 Subject Matter of Courses

In order to qualify for approval, real estate courses shall consist of a minimum of 30 classroom hours covering the following real estate subjects:

(1) Licensing Regulation — North Carolina Real Estate Licensing Law and Rules and Regulations of the Board;

(2) Glossary — real estate definitions; words and phrases;

(3) Real Estate Ownership —types of ownership (real, personal, fixtures); title (estates); transfer of title (deeds); title insurance; property descriptions (measurements, metes and bounds, plats); condominiums; zoning;

(4) Real Estate Contracts — contracts in general; statute of frauds; listing agreements; offers to purchase (escrow deposits); options; land installment contracts; leases;

(5) Law of Agency — principles of agency; brokers and salesmen as agents; duties of agent to principal; duties of principal to agent; law against discrimination; real estate management;

(6) Real Estate Financing — money market; government role in financing (FHA, VA); mortgages and deeds of trust; appraising and valuation;

(7) Real Estate Closing — closing in general; closing documents; prorations, taxes, and insurances; liens and encumbrances; hypothetical real estate closing; closing statements;

(8) Real Estate Mathematics — prorations; tax rate; area; commission; capitalization; discount; depreciation; interest; transfer tax.

History Note: Statutory Authority G.S. 93A-4(a);

Eff. February 1, 1976.

.1004 Certification of Course Completion

Schools approved by the Board shall furnish each student who successfully completes his course an official certification containing the student's name, address, date course was completed and number of classroom hours completed. Students shall be advised by the school that said certification is to be filed by the student with his application to the Board for license.

History Note: Statutory Authority G.S. 93A-3(c); 93A-4(a);

Eff. February 1, 1976.